Tarot

Made Easy

Learn How to Read and
Interpret the Cards

KIM ARNOLD

HAY HOUSE

Carlsbad, California • New York City
London • Sydney • New Delhi

Published in the United Kingdom by:
Hay House UK Ltd, The Sixth Floor, Watson House,
54 Baker Street, London W1U 7BU
Phone: +44 (0)20 3927 7290 • Fax: +44 (0)20 3927 7291
www.hayhouse.co.uk

Published in the United States of America by:
Hay House Inc., PO Box 5100, Carlsbad, CA 92018-5100
Tel: (1) 760 431 7695 or (800) 654 5126
Fax: (1) 760 431 6948 or (800) 650 5115
www.hayhouse.com

Published in Australia by:
Hay House Australia Ltd, 18/36 Ralph St, Alexandria NSW 2015
Tel: (61) 2 9669 4299; Fax: (61) 2 9669 4144
www.hayhouse.com.au

Published in India by:
Hay House Publishers India, Muskaan Complex, Plot No.3, B-2,
Vasant Kunj, New Delhi 110 070
Tel: (91) 11 4176 1620; Fax: (91) 11 4176 1630
www.hayhouse.co.in

This book was previously published under the title *Tarot* (*Hay House Basics*
series); ISBN: 978-1-78180-413-1

A catalogue record for this book is available from the British Library.

ISBN: 978-1-78817-259-2
E-book ISBN: 978-1-78817-275-2

17 16 15 14 13 12 11 10 9 8

Interior images: Africa Studio/shutterstock

Printed in the United States of America

Little could I imagine how much my life would change after I purchased my first Tarot deck. It has brought me friendship from around the world with wonderful people who share my passion. This book is dedicated to all of them.

Contents

Choosing a Deck

With so many decks on the market to choose from, I believe that you are drawn to the deck that is right for you. Many decks are based on the Rider Waite Tarot, which was published in 1910, and to this day its images are frequently used in modern Tarot.

For a beginner, I highly recommend the Rider Waite Tarot cards, as they are clear and concise, packed with information and colour, and therefore the ability to interpret from the card images is endless. Information on the Rider Waite deck is easy to obtain, and most general Tarot books and Internet sites base their information on these cards.

If you are not attracted to a Rider Waite-based deck, then find a deck that you are drawn to. Base your choice on a colourful deck in which the Minor Arcana are represented as picture cards, not just as numbers. For example, the Five of Cups will show literally five cups. As a beginner, you need something visual to help you to decipher the images.

When you buy a deck of cards, you will find that the deck calls you. New Age and metaphysical shops often have sample cards that you can look at, and, of course, you can always search online for cards that inspire you. Another benefit of looking online is that you are able to read the reviews, which will help you to make the right choice.

The feel of the cards is also important. Often, by just holding the box, you will instinctively know if they are right for you.

Ensure the visual images of the cards 'talk' to you, and you feel able to resonate with their energy, as you will find these cards much easier to read. Once you become more competent with your cards, you will start to see more and more within the images they portray.

There is an old wives' tale that states Tarot cards should be purchased as a gift. Please ignore this, as there is no better person to choose a personal deck of Tarot cards than you. Allow your instinct to guide you and I promise you will make the right choice. It is likely that as your reading skills grow, so will your Tarot card collection.

Be warned, collecting Tarot cards can be addictive!

The basic rules of Tarot

How you use your Tarot cards is up to you. If you have had a Tarot reading in the past I am sure you will notice that every reader is different, both in their technique and their ritual laying out of the cards. However, there are a few basic rules that should be observed.

Never lend your Tarot cards to anyone, as this will interfere with your energy and the energy of the cards. As you become more familiar with your cards, you will create a bond of trust between them and you. This is very powerful. The only time you should allow your Tarot cards to be touched by a third party is if you are doing a reading for them, as it is important that both your energies connect with the deck before you commence with the reading.

In order to learn the cards quickly it is important to familiarize yourself with them. Each day pick a card at random and work with it. Initially, you will find you resonate with some cards more than others. Don't worry about this, as the information will come. This book is full of effective techniques to help you to understand the cards quickly so that you will soon be able to read for yourself and others.

Always shuffle the deck thoroughly before a reading, as this acts as a cleansing ritual and allows you to connect with the cards. Shuffling the cards is an important part of Tarot reading and is covered in some depth in this book. When you finish a reading, shuffle the cards again before you return them to their box, cloth or Tarot bag, as this clears the energy from the reading ready for the next time.

When not using your cards, always wrap them in a cloth or Tarot bag or, if preferred, place them in a box. Tarot cards, as with any psychic tool, can be influenced by their surroundings. For example, if you live in a chaotic house, this energy may be picked up in your cards.

By respecting your cards and wrapping them in their own cloth, etc., you will not only establish a ritual for looking after your cards, but you will also protect them from outside energy. Some people like to place a crystal, such as an amethyst, in with their cards to disperse negativity, or add a drop of oil, such as frankincense or sandalwood, for extra protection. This is an entirely personal choice and not absolutely necessary. However, if you feel this is right for you, then why not?

Reading for yourself, friends and relatives

People often ask if it is ok to read for yourself, and the answer is yes, absolutely! The negative side of doing your own reading is that you are most likely to interpret what you want rather than listen to the message the cards are giving you, particularly if you are not seeing the answer you desire. I suggest that you ask a 'closed' question by being very specific and putting in a time reference. For example, 'Will I change my job?' is an open question. You may well change your job in 10 years' time, but if the question is relevant to you now, then you need to include a time limit with the question. Therefore, you should rephrase the question to something such as 'Will I change my job within the next six months?' Then just lay one card for guidance – this can be a very powerful way to get straight to the point.

Reading for those close to you, such as family or friends, can be a bit tricky. It is likely you will be aware of issues surrounding them, and may unconsciously add your opinion rather than being objective. Again, it is a good idea to help with guidance through short readings, and laying one to three cards until you are more familiar with the cards and their meanings.

Who is the querent?

The word querent comes from the word 'query' and refers to the person asking a question of the cards. Sometimes the querent can also be known as the 'seeker'. These are both familiar terms for anyone looking for answers through divination.

Psychic protection

Personally, I do not use psychic protection before using my cards. However, some people feel this is necessary and perform short rituals before commencing a reading.

Using a ritual for protection can be as simple as saying a prayer or a blessing. If you feel the need to do something more elaborate, you could try a short meditation and bring in the white light of protection to surround you. Lighting a candle or having crystals nearby when reading can, for some, enhance psychic energy. However, if this does not seem necessary, then don't. Always trust your intuition when reading the cards – you will rarely be wrong.

Responsibility

It is a fact that most people have a Tarot reading when they are experiencing a crisis and feeling vulnerable, or are at a crossroads in their life and looking for guidance. Many seekers are looking for answers to a specific question.

Reading the Tarot is a very responsible job, and vulnerable people may take every word you say literally. While it is important that you are confident with the cards before reading for others, it is equally important to remind the client that they have free will, and that the messages from the cards are not set in stone.

When I do a reading for a new client, I always mention before I begin that they should not worry if the Death card comes out, as it will indicate a major change, not a physical death. A little knowledge can be a dangerous thing. If a client sees the Death card in their reading, they may focus on this even if positive cards surround it.

It is important to read responsibly. There are many ways to answer questions and share information. Advice given through the cards may be life changing for some. It is therefore important to remember that everyone has free will in order to make their own changes, should they need to. The cards are for guidance, but our destiny is ours alone.

Tarot – where it all began

It is believed that the word 'Tarot' comes from the River Taro in Northern Italy, where the popular game of Tarocchi was played in the early fifteenth century. Tarot was not originally designed as a tool for divination, but as a card game that became popular as a fortune-telling aid in the late eighteenth century.

There have been many stories as to the origins of Tarot. Some believe it evolved in Egypt, or it was bought to Europe by the travelling Gypsies.

A Swiss clergyman, Antoine Court de Gébelin, who published *Le Monde Primitif*, a study of religious symbolism, believed that Gypsies were the descendants of the Ancient Egyptians, and that they were the first to use Tarot cards for divination. However, there is no proof to support this theory.

The first known Tarot deck of 78 cards was discovered in Italy in 1442. This is confirmed by the court records in Ferrara, Italy, and is the first true evidence of their existence. In the fifteenth century, Tarot cards were hand painted and were owned only by the wealthy. During this period they were used for gaming, not for fortune telling. Often the images included members of the family, which provides a glimpse into the lives of the nobility during this period.

From the late eighteenth century to present day, Tarot has evolved far beyond being a tool for fortune telling. Aside from divination, Tarot cards are also used for meditation, mind mapping and spiritual and personal guidance.

As Tarot readings become mainstream, people from all walks of life are turning to the Tarot for guidance in decision-making. In the past, I have been employed by stock exchanges around the world, which made major decisions on the turn of a card. It is important to stress that everyone has free will, and even if the advice offered by a Tarot card is perfectly clear, it is still your choice whether to follow it or to make your own decision.

The biggest influence in modern Tarot is the Rider Waite Tarot deck. It was created by the mystic Arthur Edward Waite and the artist, illustrator and writer Pamela Colman Smith (known as Pixie), and was published in 1910. The legacy of the deck continues to thrive today, and many modern decks still use much of the early Rider Waite symbolism.

Part I

THE MAJOR ARCANA

The 22 cards of the Major Arcana form the foundation of a Tarot deck. Their symbolism can provide important spiritual lessons.

Chapter 1

Cards of the Major Arcana

A Tarot deck comprises 78 picture cards, which are interpreted by the reader in different ways. Their reading and interpretation depends on how many cards are drawn, and in what position they lay within the spread.

Despite popular belief, there are no good and bad cards in Tarot. Each card has its merits, and depicts our path and options at the time of the reading.

A deck comprises of 22 Major Arcana and 56 Minor Arcana cards. The Minor Arcana has four suits commonly known as Pentacles (or Coins), Swords, Wands (or Batons) and Cups. Each suit has four Court cards, known as the Page, Knight, Queen and King.

The 22 Major Arcana cards (sometimes called Trump cards) relate to the major issues in our lives, and predominately focus on where we are on our life journey.

Each Major Arcana card has a name and a number, which are significant in a reading. Their messages are powerful and meaningful. If Major Arcana cards dominate a reading, it suggests the querent or seeker has some major issues to deal with. Minor Arcana cards within a reading will bring balance and direction. As we combine the Major and Minor Arcana cards together, they will offer clear guidance relating to the issues surrounding the querent.

The images within Tarot are universal and they can be read by anyone. Most people start off with intuitive readings. When you do this it is likely you are tapping into your psychic ability as you connect with the cards. However, as you become more familiar with the cards and study them in greater depth, you will be able to add layers of information and enhance the information given in a reading.

Understanding the 'fear' cards

Death, The Devil, The Tower and The Moon

It is important to remember that Tarot is a divination tool. Its purpose is to help guide you on your path, and through situations in which you may not be able to see a positive ending.

There are a few cards in the Tarot deck that have a negative image. I have lost count of the number of times I have told people I am a Tarot reader and have seen an expression of fear spread across their face. Another common response is that they would never have a reading in case the Death card appeared.

The often-dreaded Death card rarely predicts physical death, and indeed it would take a particular sequence of cards to signify this. The Death card predicts a closure and the end of a situation. If a client is dealing with a serious issue, I silently ask that the Death card appears, as it brings the message that an end to the issue is near, and change is inevitable. This is often only for the better – as old doors close, new opportunities can present themselves.

The Devil card represents unhealthy attachments. It is likely that if the Devil appears in your reading, you are in a situation in which you no longer wish to be. Ask yourself if you feel in control, or if a person or situation is controlling you. The message from this card advises you to break free from the restrictions that bind you, and to take positive steps to change a situation in your life.

The Tower card has an image of a burning tower being struck by lightning. This card relates to sudden change and can be very cathartic. Often we need a lightning-bolt moment to shift old negative energy and patterns, and encourage us to let go and start again.

The Moon card warns us that we have to be careful of gossip, lies and deceit. Trust your instincts when the Moon appears, as you will rarely be wrong.

These are just a few of the Major Arcana cards that may cause concern. More often than not there is nothing to worry about.

Each card is influenced by the card or cards that surround it in a reading. There is always a positive message to be found in any card – even if it means dealing with a situation we'd rather avoid, it always comes right in the end.

0 The Fool

Key words: Potential, choices, innocence, new beginnings

Image: A young man stands on the edge of a precipice carrying his worldly possessions. A dog barks at his feet, warning him of the dangers that may lie ahead.

The Fool appears in a reading when the querent (seeker) is ready for change. This card is associated with the start of a new journey or venture. There is an air of innocence about this card, and it is important that your feet are firmly on the ground before you take the next step. The presence of the Fool energy around you implies that the changes ahead have an element of risk attached to them, or that you are hesitant about making a decision. However, it is likely that now is the right time to make major changes, and you are ready to throw caution to the wind and take a leap of faith. If you are feeling restricted, or that you have been stuck in a rut, now is the right time to leave your comfort zone behind and look for new opportunities.

The Fool has great ambitions and is looking forwards to the next step of his journey. However, it may be that you are blinded by the positive aspects of what lies ahead so it is important that, before you make a major decision, you take the time to weigh up all of your options.

The Fool's journey is often full of potential, but how you handle your options will decide whether this has a positive or negative outcome. The Fool encourages us to confront our fears, which is something you may feel reluctant to do, but you need to overcome this and act for the benefit of your emotional and physical wellbeing.

You are likely to be feeling impulsive and looking forwards to a new challenge. This can be an inspiring and adventurous time, but make sure you are prepared for what lies ahead.

One thing is certain: you are ready for change when the Fool appears. Just be prepared to take some time to weigh up the pros and cons before you leap into the unknown, and remember that this can be a phase that is full of new adventures and opportunities.

Reversed: Foolish, reckless, taking risks

Affirmation: *'My life is an adventure. I ask for guidance so that the opportunity to follow my true path becomes clear to me.'*

I The Magician

Key words: Resources, manifestation, action

Image: The Magician's table holds the tools of the four suits: a coin/pentacle (money), a sword (ideas), a cup (emotions) and a wand (creativity). These items represent everything you need to make your dreams reality. He points at heaven and the Earth, looking for both spiritual and earthly balance.

If you are looking for change, such as a new relationship, new career, a need to make more money or progress with an idea, then the Magician will help you to manifest your dreams. The desire to take action rather than just thinking about ideas will feel more urgent now and your energy levels will be high.

It is important to focus on your goal and not be distracted by random opportunities that are not beneficial to you at this time.

The energy of this powerful card suggests that the timing is right for you to make major decisions and use your resources to focus on achieving the desired outcome. The Magician will help you to focus on all you need to move things forwards. You may have been feeling restless of late, but you will start to feel your energy rise as the Magician's magic is ready to work with you. Start to plan how you will make progress, and if it is right for you, you will see ideas fall effortlessly into place. The Magician represents spiritual and earthly balance, and when these combinations are in harmony, you will feel at peace with yourself and life will flow more freely. This is part of the Magician's strength.

It is time to seize the moment and be proactive in moving forwards with your ideas.

The Magician is often perceived as a lucky card. However, early Tarot decks portrayed him as a trickster, so this is also a warning to be careful about who you involve in your plans as they may not be all they seem.

Trust your intuition and be reassured that the energy of this card will provide you with all you need.

Reversed: Insecurity, control

Affirmation: *'I have all that I need to accomplish my goals; I do not have to follow a path that is not true to me.'*

II The High Priestess

Key words: Intuition, wisdom, knowledge

Image: The High Priestess sits between two pillars – one black and one white – at the entrance to a temple. She has a crescent moon at her feet, images of pomegranates behind her, and she wears a large cross. These are all symbols of religion and spirituality. She hides the Torah, a scroll of secrets within her cloak.

The High Priestess reminds us that the most powerful gift we have is our intuition. If you have pulled this card, her message is that you are likely not to be heeding yours. How many times have you thought to yourself, *I knew I should have done this or that,* but you allowed logic to override what your instinct was telling you?

The High Priestess is sometimes known as the mediator, so you may currently find yourself in a situation that needs some balance. Do not allow yourself to be in a situation in which you are manipulated. Your inner voice is telling you what you need to know and you must learn to trust your own instincts. You may feel that you are not speaking your truth and having to hold your tongue. If you find it difficult to express your anger, worries or needs, then connect with the High Priestess, as her message is to trust your feelings. Ask yourself why you are having such difficulty in dealing with this situation and allow her guidance to flow.

The High Priestess encourages us to meditate, or to find some time in our day to be at peace with ourselves. By practising quiet time, you will notice your own intuition and psychic abilities becoming stronger, and you will learn to recognize your instincts as a positive voice within you. The High Priestess is reminding you to listen to your deep inner feelings. Intuition is a primal instinct. We are all born intuitive, so reconnect with yourself. Read, use cards, buy a spiritual magazine, join a group, meditate – whatever you decide – but it is recommended that you take steps to help yourself to become more confident and learn to distinguish the difference between your thoughts and a psychic message.

Do not involve yourself in gossip or situations that are not of your concern. The High Priestess is wisely advising you to step back and observe rather than allowing yourself to be dragged into a situation that does not concern you.

Reversed: Secrets, manipulation

Affirmation: *'I trust and follow my intuition; I receive the answers I am looking for.'*

III The Empress

THE EMPRESS.

Key words: Fertility, creativity, mother, kindness

Image: The Empress sits on cushions, surrounded by a lush landscape representing the abundance of Mother Nature. She is pregnant, a symbol of new life and new beginnings. The Empress is a mother figure; she represents a pregnancy, a birth or the creation of a new project.

This is a card of abundance, a time of growth and beauty. You may feel the urge to make personal changes: try a new hairstyle or join a gym. This energy can be extended to the home – perhaps it is time to redecorate or have work done?

The Empress loves beautiful things and will do all she can to create a peaceful and loving environment. She may extend her ideas to others, even if her opinion has not been asked for. She is nurturing and motherly; however, sometimes can overstep the mark, not realizing her energy can be quite overbearing and powerful. The need to be aware of your strengths and weaknesses is apparent now.

If you are a mother/daughter/sister, you may be feeling particularly overprotective towards your family. You are often the voice of reason and try to avert family disharmony whenever possible. However, be sure your advice is required before voicing your opinion as you may be accused of interfering.

The timing is perfect for planting the seeds for future growth, as a new venture may be on the horizon. If you have been thinking about branching out on your own, this is a good time to set the wheels in motion. If you feel you are not quite ready for a major change, there is no harm in seeking advice and letting the universe know you mean business. Taking the first step is important now – your energy and good mood are contagious and there is a confident air around you. This suggests that whatever you put your mind to will be the start of something special.

The Empress loves the good life, not necessarily in a monetary sense, but through feeling loved and loving others. However, don't allow people to become dependent on you. Your support can sometimes be misinterpreted and you may find yourself being overwhelmed with other people's problems.

Reversed: indecisiveness, lack of personal care

Affirmation: *'Abundance and creativity are within my grasp; I believe in myself.'*

IV The Emperor

Key words: Authority, stability, structure, advice

Image: The Emperor sits upon a stone throne. He has no need for abundant surroundings as his strength and stature speak for themselves. His red clothes and metal boots relate to authority.

The Emperor represents a male figure whom we respect, such as a teacher, a lawyer, a doctor, a boss or a financial advisor. He has an air of authority about him and in some cases can be a father figure or an older man.

It is likely you will be seeking guidance from the Emperor either now or in the near future. His energy will help you to organize random thoughts and structure your priorities.

If you are in a situation where you are battling with authority, this card reminds you of your own strengths. The power of this card suggests that as long as you have done your homework and your facts are clear, you will not lose an argument. It is important that you stay true to your convictions and not allow your thoughts and ideas to be dismissed by someone with a strong personality. Stand your ground.

The Emperor represents structure and stability, and suggests it is time for you to put your life in order. This is a good time to clear the clutter, both physically and emotionally. Taking control of the issues that surround you will echo the start of a new and positive phase in your life.

If you are starting new projects, you may find overthinking is clouding your judgement. Take a deep breath, regroup and start to build a solid foundation with which to work, even if it means things take a little longer. In order to reach your goals you need time to tie up loose ends, and confront the issues you have been putting off. The Emperor's energy will help you to create order. Be more assertive – you can do it! You just need to believe in yourself.

The Emperor will help bring stability to any chaos that may be around you. He may represent a third party, a person of trust and knowledge, who will advise you without prejudice.

Throughout history, the Emperor has been a figure of leadership. Trust his guidance, he is wise and experienced; it is likely he will give you fair and sound advice.

Reversed: Poor judgement, lack of direction

Affirmation: *'I have the power to be successful. I am assertive.'*

V The Hierophant

Key words: Spiritual, religion, tradition

Image: The Hierophant or pope is the holy leader. Two servants sit at his feet waiting for instructions. The crossed keys can represent the keys with which to open the door of opportunity.

The Hierophant card can represent a new path and encourages us to be open to ideas and opinions that we may have previously dismissed. If you are someone who is not open-minded, this card asks that you try to be more flexible as you may miss out on an important opportunity. Although this card connects with spirituality, personal life events may be making you unsettled right now and reassurance is needed.

The urge to be part of something more satisfying than you are currently experiencing will feel necessary at this stage of your life. There is a sense of getting out there and showing the world who you are and what you can do.

If you have been raised within a religious structure, you might be questioning what you have known. A pull and desire to research more about other religions and cultures may feature prominently now. Your own psychic awareness is becoming stronger, and it is likely you are feeling the need to join a spiritual group or you are seeking a teacher to help develop your psychic gift.

You have reached a spiritual crossroads and will find that opportunities for personal development will come to you. It is important to trust your intuition and be connected with like-minded people to develop and learn. Groups, associations, workshops and classes may be of interest now.

The Hierophant may appear physically in your life as a wise friend or teacher. However he manifests in your life, this is an important period for you.

A personal journey of learning, knowledge and wisdom; exploring traditions of ancient crafts; meditating and finding peace within yourself –whatever is in store for you now, this will be one of the most significant periods in your life.

This is a card of wisdom, so listen to your teachers and those who are already on a spiritual path. Take from them what you need and leave alone what does not sit right with you. Your own intuition will guide you as to what is right and wrong.

Reversed: Judgemental, loss of faith, restriction

Affirmation: *'I balance my spiritual and physical needs by making time for myself.'*

VI The Lovers

Key words: Love, harmony, union

Image: Adam and Eve stand naked in front of the tree of life and the tree of forbidden fruit, representing vulnerability. The Archangel Raphael appears above them.

The Lovers can have many interpretations in a reading. If you are looking for love, it can suggest a partner is not far away. If you are in a relationship, it can represent a deeper commitment. It can also represent a passion or love for a new project. I often see this as a card representing close family issues.

This card is always influenced by the cards that surround it. If you are in a long-term relationship, there may be a change of dynamics and the surrounding cards will decipher whether this is for better or worse. For example, if the Lovers appear next to the Sun card, it would suggest news of an engagement or marriage. But if it appears next to the Moon card, it may suggest deceit or betrayal.

The Lovers' energy can be passionate and joyful. On the negative side, it can represent a third person within the relationship. This is not to suggest that it is always deceitful – instead it may relate to someone who is overly demanding, and therefore distracting you from what is important right now. Be careful not to neglect those who need your love and attention most. Do not allow resentment of another person to overshadow all that is good in your life at this time.

You may be looking at a relationship in a different light, either searching for greater commitment or possibly to release yourself from restrictions you may be feeling. This card suggests it is time to think about your choices and make decisions for your long-term emotional wellbeing.

In some Tarot decks the Archangel Raphael is prominently featured in the Lovers card between the man and the woman (Adam and Eve). As the Archangel of love and healing, his message is to remind you to take care and to learn to love yourself. If your relationship has experienced a rough patch and needs extra attention at this time, you can call upon Raphael for guidance. He will also bring into your life the strength of healing and support.

Ultimately, the Lovers is a card of commitment, love and bonding.

Reversed: Separation, disharmony

Affirmation: *'I welcome new people into my life and attract those who are right for me.'*

VII The Chariot

Key words: Decisions, choices, taking control

Image: A soldier stands in his chariot, deciding in which direction to go. The two sphinxes – one black, one white – are both at an angle; the destiny is uncertain. The sphinxes are not tethered to the chariot, symbolizing the soldier has free will to go wherever he chooses.

The Chariot represents a period of uncertainty. If you feel that the world is working against you, the current path you have chosen may be a karmic lesson – something that needs to be resolved in order for you to move on. The challenges you are faced with represent only a minor upheaval, so it is important that you do not blow things out of proportion. The matter in hand can be dealt with swiftly and calmly as long as you do not let your emotions take over.

Although this may sound negative, the Chariot is, in fact, quite a positive card. The final outcome is often for the best, even if it feels like the road to get there was challenging and full of obstacles. You will feel a great sense of achievement as you reach the final hurdle, and know that you have worked hard to battle against the odds.

The Chariot can sometimes represent physical movement, such as a new career opportunity or a house move. The transition may not be as smooth as you hoped, but if this move is right for you, you will get there in the end.

There is almost certainly an anticipation of inevitable change happening around you. In some part, you may feel you have no choice in the matter, but the Chariot is all about choices and decisions, and the need to take control of a situation as well as not allowing yourself to be swept away with the tide of suggestions that do not feel right to you. You are stronger than you think, and do not have to do anything you do not wish to.

The Chariot reminds you of your own strength, so trust your intuition – it will not let you down. Once you are able to connect with your inner self, you will know that whatever you choose to do at this time is within your reach. Yes, it may be uncomfortable for a while – you are coming out of your comfort zone – so embrace it. The end result will be well worth a short period of struggle.

Reversed: Out of control, conflict

Affirmation: *'I have choices, and I trust my intuition to make the decision that is right for me.'*

VIII Strength

Key words: Courage, inner strength, discipline

Image: A woman gently holds open the mouth of a lion. She has no fear. The figure above her head is the infinity symbol, and her white robe is a symbol of innocence.

The Strength card often appears when the querent has felt they have had to deal with difficult circumstances beyond their control. If you have found the need to bite your tongue or even lash out, this card reminds you that you have the control to deal with a situation. There are two very different sides to this card. Ask yourself how much power the situation calls for. Are you coming across as overly passive or too aggressive? Would a gentle hand be more effective than a powerful push? Strength urges us to find the appropriate level of energy needed to handle the events confronting us.

This card represents feminine energy and, ultimately, compassion and kindness. You may have recently experienced a situation in which you needed to be strong, not only for yourself but also possibly for another person.

It is likely you are emerging from a challenging situation. When the Strength card appears, we find our inner strength. Whatever is currently going on in your life, you should feel happy that you have done all you can do. This card reminds us that finding inner strength is sometimes the most difficult challenge we face. The strength to believe in yourself, the strength to follow your dreams, is calling you now.

This is a time to bring your attributes into balance: if you are feeling angry, find a way to let that anger go; if you are feeling fearful, look at ways to overcome this; if you are facing a challenge, this card will see you through to the end. The message is clear – you need not worry. All you need to make a better life is within you. It is time to take on the challenges you have been dreading. You are strong enough to face your fears. It is unlikely things will change overnight, but taking small steps towards your goal each day will help you become brave and fearless in all you do.

There is an air of achievement surrounding the Strength card, a feeling of knowing your own self worth. You are admired for all you do, even if it sometimes feels that you are not appreciated.

Reversed: Weakness, overwhelmed by situations

Affirmation: *'I have the strength to overcome any obstacles.'*

IX The Hermit

Key words: Solitude, retreat, meditation

Image: The Hermit stands on top of a mountain holding a lit lantern to show him the way forwards. He steadies himself with a staff as he contemplates his next move.

The Hermit card indicates a time for personal reflection. It is a card of requiring peace and quiet, and offers you a chance to think and regroup if you are feeling overwhelmed by the pressures of everyday life. New opportunities are waiting for you, but if life has been too busy for you to see your true potential, then listen to the Hermit's message.

This is a time in your life where the answers you are looking for cannot be bought, as they are little to do with the material world. There are changes going on within you that can only be found by looking inwards. The Hermit energy requires you to observe and take your time before making decisions. Don't do anything in haste at this time; there is no urgency. If you are feeling overwhelmed by other people's demands, then it is time for you to step back and encourage them to find their own path, which does not place any burden upon you.

The term 'soul searching' is often associated with the Hermit, a time of revaluation of where your life is right now. Perhaps you have been doing too much lately and need to take some time out? This card can relate to studying, the ability to lose yourself in something that interests you. This is a good time to take on new interests, particularly those that allow you to indulge in your own company.

The Hermit card suggests you are wise beyond your years, even if you don't always feel this. The frantic life you are currently living needs some balance. This would be a good time to meditate, to reconnect with your inner soul and with the stillness within, which will allow you to focus and move forwards.

One thing for sure is that you need to have space and time to yourself. If a change of scenery is not possible at this time, a long walk in the park or on the beach will have the desired effect. Read, listen to music, and, most importantly, listen to what your body needs.

Reversed: Introvert, loneliness

Affirmation: *'Taking time out is an option, I need to create calm in my life.'*

X Wheel of Fortune

Key words: Change, finances, luck

Image: The wheel is surrounded by four images of earth, air, fire and water, which are represented by four signs of the zodiac. A sphinx sits at the top of the wheel and Anubis, (a jackal-headed god associated with mummification and the afterlife in ancient Egypt) reclines below; a snake appears on the left side.

The Wheel of Fortune indicates a change of events, often for the better. As the wheel turns, it shifts the energy around you and, depending on which cards surround the Wheel of Fortune, determines whether this is negative or positive. Now is a good time to step out of your comfort zone and take action – under the energy of the Wheel of Fortune the odds are usually in your favour. We often associate this card with money, but in fact it represents much more. It is the only card in Tarot that clearly shows the four virtues, represented by earth, air, fire and water. Therefore it can represent any area in your life: money, emotional stability, ideas or work.

The Wheel of Fortune is often seen as a lucky card and indicates a good time to act on hunches and instinct. However, it is important to remember the wheel can turn either way, and represents life's ups and downs. Maybe you feel you have been on an emotional roller coaster ride of late, and you are now entering a period in which you are feeling more in control.

This card is associated with good luck and fortune, and can predict unexpected positive events, even a windfall. Look out for opportunities that appear from nowhere as Lady Luck is on your side and will present new and exciting options to you.

If you have been struggling with your finances, money may be about to appear from an unexpected source. Look at clearing your clutter – there could be items of value sitting right under your nose.

The Wheel of Fortune indicates situations going full circle. If you have loose ends to tie up, the cycle to completing these is coming to an end. Sometimes this card has karmic implications. If it feels like the wheel has been spinning endlessly and your life has been out of control, things will now begin to become calmer. This is a good time to put in extra effort to manifest whatever you desire.

Reversed: Failure, bad luck

Affirmation: *'I attract abundance into my life; money and good fortune flow freely to me.'*

XI Justice

Key words: Balance, truth, justice

Image: A sword in her right hand represents logic; the scales in her left represent intuition. The red robes are symbolic of power.

The Justice card relates to law, order and balance. It can represent legal matters, settling disputes, the signing of documents or contracts, or literally the restoration balance in your life. If you feel you have been the victim of an injustice, this card will help you to make the right choices in rebalancing the scales.

One of the main aspects of Justice is truth: speaking your truth and trusting your instinct with any information you are being given. If you are in a moral dilemma, listen to your instincts regarding how to proceed without compromising your integrity.

This card implies that it is not only you who may have to take responsibility for your actions, but also someone around you. If you are dealing with a dispute, make sure you are confident that all the facts you have are accurate. It is extremely important you read the small print in any documentation.

With the Justice card in your reading, the truth will come out and there is nowhere to hide. If you have done everything by the book and sought advice where required, this card suggests a favourable outcome.

If you are embarking on a new relationship or partnership, Justice can indicate an excellent match. However, with any business decisions being made at this time, be sure you have discussed and agreed all aspects of your roles, as any discrepancies missed now could lead to future disagreements.

Justice can imply an imbalance emotionally or physically, or both. It is time to look at the structure of your routine. Are you doing too much? You need to learn how to manage your life better so that you are in harmony with all that is around you. It is important to have balance both physically and spiritually. If you are able to achieve this, then your heart and soul are in harmony and life will flow with ease.

The Justice card will help restore balance in all that is wrong in your life. It will also give you the courage to put the past behind you.

Reversed: Unfairness, accusations

Affirmation: *'Integrity and balance are important to me; I work towards creating harmony in my life.'*

XII The Hanged Man

Key words: Suspension, martyrdom, release

Image: A man hangs upside down, suspended from a tree. The bright yellow light around his head is a symbol of martyrdom.

The Hanged Man suggests you are experiencing a frustrating period in your life; nothing is flowing and whatever you try to do is taking more effort than should be necessary. You may well find that however hard you try to move a situation forwards: you feel you are hitting your head against a brick wall. The Hanged Man appears now for good reason; his message is to look again at the issues that are not flowing for you. Is everything where it needs to be? More importantly, is the timing right for you?

This card encourages us to look at a situation from another angle. Things are rarely just black or white, but your views may be fixed, and perhaps you are not willing to compromise to reach a resolution. If you are looking to resolve an issue quickly, compromise might be the only way forwards. It is likely a problem is causing you stress, which is also hindering your ability to think clearly. Everything around you is in suspension, the sooner you face up to the facts and are able to begin to deal with the problems, the sooner everything in your life will begin to flow.

You may be finding it hard to make a decision, feeling that whatever choice you make might not be right. Therefore, you prefer to do nothing, but you know at some point you have to take a deep breath and move things forwards. By doing nothing you are only delaying the outcome.

There is an air of stubbornness about the Hanged Man; some say he is the card of martyrdom. However, it is important to remember that nothing is ever achieved by standing still (or hanging around, as the Hanged Man is depicted). By making a small sacrifice now could lead to huge rewards later.

However, if you feel there really is nothing you can do to break the frustration, then allow yourself to move on. Maybe you are not meant to push issues, so let the universe decide when the changes should occur.

Reversed: Indecision and lack of effort

Affirmation: *'This time of suspension gives me the time and opportunity to focus on what is truly important right now.'*

XIII Death

Key words: Transformation, change, endings and beginnings

Image: A skeleton in armour rides a white horse, leaving devastation behind him. He holds a flag of the white rose declaring peace; a holy man waits in prayer as the sun rises behind him.

The Death card does not mean physical death, but rather a transformation. However, the negative aspect of this card is that we may experience a difficult emotional phase before we realize that all was meant to be.

Death can indicate a change in your old self. Maybe you have had the trauma of a break-up of a relationship and are beginning to see light at the end of the tunnel. Death can be something as simple as a change of lifestyle or a major shift in your life such as redundancy, retirement, a new job or living arrangements, or an illness in someone close. All these events can be typical Death-card scenarios.

This card can be one of the most fruitful cards in the deck. It is symbolic of the ending of a major phase that will in turn bring about the beginning of something far more valuable and important in the long term.

If you have experienced a stressful period, then the Death card is a welcome sight in a reading. Many people fear the Death card, but the reality is that we experience endings all the time. There is nothing to fear – as one door closes, another really does open.

Usually, when the Death card appears, we have very little choice in a matter. You may fight hard against change, but give it time. Everything happens for a reason, and in the end you will see that it is right for you.

Do not worry if the Death card appears in a reading. This phase in your life is changing, and possibly quite dramatically. There is no doubt that something has to shift. Although a closure may feel frightening, there is likely to be improvement as new opportunities arise.

Just to clarify, to see a physical death in Tarot would require a sequence of specific cards. My belief is there is no benefit in predicting death. Life is for living and we should make the most of every moment!

Reversed: Stagnant, inability to move on

Affirmation: *'Transformation is part of my life's journey; new doors are opening for me as I release the past.'*

XIV Temperance

Key words: Balance, patience, healing

Image: The Archangel Michael stands at the edge of a lake dipping his toe in the water. He holds two chalices, tipping water from one to the other. The land around is lush, and the sun rises in the distance.

Temperance will help you to bring balance and harmony into a situation that requires a decision. It is likely you are undecided about which way you should go, and prone to too much dithering, weighing up the emotional pros and cons before deciding what action to take.

You may be toying with new ideas and how you can turn them into reality, so take your time before committing to final decisions. There is much to think about, and you may just need to dip your toe in before overextending yourself. If there is an option to test the water, then it is highly recommended that you do so. Patience is a virtue, but don't wait too long before making a decision. All thought and no action will only delay what is right for you now.

Temperance brings an optimistic air about it. This energy comes through life lessons. It may be that you have experienced difficult challenges in your past, but you have learned so much on a personal level; it is the confidence gained from dealing with turmoil that now gives you the strength to face almost anything.

There is a quiet, gentle confidence about you during this phase. Whatever you choose to do, follow your intuition for the right guidance.

Often Temperance is depicted by an image of the Archangel Michael, the Angel of Protection. If you have had health issues, you should now be on the mend or dealing with illness in a positive way. You need to make yourself a priority, as you have been so busy looking after everyone else you may have neglected your own needs. You have a big, kind heart, but it is time to redress the balance and be kind to yourself. Healing is needed to enable you to reconnect with yourself and others.

Try putting yourself at the top of your 'important person' list and learn to say no to those who take advantage of your good nature.

Reversed: Imbalance and hostility

Affirmation: *'I can create harmony in any situation. I have all I need to achieve my goals.'*

XV The Devil

Key words: Entrapment, slavery, materialism

Image: A man and a woman, Adam and Eve, stand naked with chains around their necks. Look closely and you will see the chains are large enough to be removed. The Devil appears as half man, half goat; his dark and forceful presence dominates the card.

The Devil card suggests you may be overburdened with responsibility or in a situation you feel unable to change. An example might be that you are in a job you dislike, or in an unhappy relationship that you feel unable to leave. Walking away from a job or relationship that is no longer working for you takes huge courage, but the chains of the Devil confirm that you are not happy with your situation.

The Devil may appear when a strong personality has been allowed to dominate thoughts and actions. There is a feeling that you are not in control of your destiny, and that someone else is dictating it. If this is the case, you need to work on your confidence issues.

Although frequently thought of as a negative card, the Devil does offer you choices. However, it is often 'Hobson's Choice' because, whichever way you turn, it seems that the alternative options are no better than what you are already dealing with. The saying 'better the devil you know, than the devil you don't', rings true when we choose to stay in a negative situation for all the wrong reasons.

If you are not happy with your life, then you need to look at how you can change things. You do not have to make any major decisions just now, but maybe begin to look at your options and how you may find alternative solutions to prepare for a better future. However, make sure that the ties that bind you are not of your own making.

The Devil can also indicate overindulgence and addictions. It is time to take control if you are overeating, drinking too much or even dabbling in drugs. You need a positive distraction and to take action now. Do not allow the energy of the Devil card to tempt you to a place of no return.

Reversed: Overcoming obstacles, letting go

Affirmation: *'I release all negative restrictions around me. I take responsibility for my actions and encourage light and harmony into my life.'*

XVI The Tower

THE TOWER.

Key words: Destruction, challenges, turmoil

Image: Lightning strikes the tower, dark clouds and fire emerge from the image and two people fall aimlessly to the ground. Everything appears to be out of control.

When the Tower card turns up in a reading, the impact is often quick and devastating. Look closely at this card and you will see the Tower was not built on strong foundations in the first place. It is likely you are facing a situation that is causing you concern. Whatever is going on in your life right now was always a disaster waiting to happen. You may be experiencing sudden and unexpected changes because you rushed into a situation without weighing up the negative aspects. It is, however, important now to focus on the positive. Whatever has changed will set you free and allow you to start again with new-found wisdom and enthusiasm.

It may be that nothing at this time has changed significantly; in which case, you need to look at what you are struggling with. If something in your life is taking too much effort for no personal gain either emotionally or physically, then it is time to redress the balance.

The Tower in a reading predicts that something will break if not dealt with and no action is taken. This is not a good time to bury your head in the sand – the quicker you take action the less impact the Tower will have when it falls.

The Tower can be a cathartic card. Whatever has changed will be a life-long lesson for you, although it may not seem like a good thing at the time. Your whole outlook on life will alter because of this period in your life. It may have been a challenging period, but the lessons you have learned will far outweigh any negatives.

Take a deep breath and recognize that the opportunity to make something good out of your situation will soon become clear. Karmic debt has been rebalanced and you will be stronger and more capable of getting things right in the next stage of your life. Often the Tower needs to fall in order to rebuild and start over.

Reversed: Avoiding change, averting disaster

Affirmation: *'I reorganize my life and let go of the past. Positive experiences come out of every challenge I face.'*

XVII The Star

Key words: Hope, inspiration, opportunity

Image: A naked woman pours healing water from two containers, one into a pool and the other onto the ground. There are seven white stars above her head, representing the seven chakras and the need for balance.

Symbolically, she is pouring away the old way of life and waiting for new opportunities to emerge. It is time for you to let go of old emotional baggage and embrace the new day. If you have recently been through a difficult period in your life, things are about to get a whole lot better. The healing process is in full swing, and you will find your energy lifted and your outlook more positive.

There is a gentle energy that relates to this card. Nothing is rushed, as your life is at long last going with the flow. Things are soon to change for the better. This is an inspiring period in your life and new ideas are about to become reality. Relationships feel balanced and there is an air about you that indicates this is your time to receive abundance from the universe.

This card can also signify a creative period in your life; hidden skills will start to surface and you will realize that you are more self-sufficient than you thought. Often under this influence, we become more connected with our spirituality. When you learn to trust your inner voice, you will feel more connected to your senses as your intuition and psychic skills become more apparent. You are a natural healer and may be looking to study alternative therapy or join a spiritual group. You are less worried about the physical world and any problems you might be facing. You may be feeling generous with your time or even money, rebalancing relationships where someone has helped you in the past; you are now in a position to return the favour.

There is an air of calm about you and you are ready to focus on new ideas. If there is something you have always wanted to do but not felt you have had the confidence to pursue, then now is an excellent time to start the ball rolling.

Reversed: Unfulfilled desires, imbalance

Affirmation: *'Opportunity and optimism surround me. I embrace the future with excitement.'*

XVIII The Moon

Key words: Deceit, illusion, emotions

Image: A dog and a wolf howl at the moon sending out a warning. A crayfish emerges from the water representing the energy of the astrological water signs of Pisces, Scorpio and Cancer.

The Moon card warns of deception and confusion. This is an important time for you to trust your instincts, as your perception will be high now. If you are experiencing mood swings and anxiety, they will pass; allow yourself to go with the flow. If you can meditate, do so. It will help to calm your mind. Check out the moon phase when you pull this card. If we are approaching a new moon, it is time to make new plans. If a full moon is near, it is time to release any negative emotions and take action.

We associate this card with deceit, so be careful whom you are sharing your secrets with, as they may not be as loyal as you first thought. If you are hiding something you need to be extra careful during this influence, as the Moon card has ways of bringing hidden issues to the surface. If secrets are being shared with you, be sure you want to be the keeper as this may have consequences.

This is a good time to look at your past behaviour. Has something from your past affected who you are now, or a situation you find yourself in? There is often much soul-searching under the Moon influence. You need to pay attention to your intuition. It is likely you are ignoring your inner voice, but don't dismiss this as an important message is trying to guide you.

If you are asking a question about relationships, the Moon card can suggest deception, or it may be that you are unsure if a relationship is right for you. You may be making decisions that affect your emotional wellbeing. Boundaries need to be put in place as a feeling of insecurity is causing you concern. Whatever the issues, trust your gut feelings. Look at your negative habits or overindulgences and how you can break these destructive patterns.

Your dream state may be heightened under this influence. Answers and guidance to inner conflicts, which need to be addressed, are often sent via our dreams.

Reversed: Caution, warning

Affirmation: *'I shift this unsettled energy and ask for clear guidance to help achieve this.'*

XIX The Sun

Key words: Happiness, harmony, love

Image: A naked baby rides a white horse representing innocence and joy. The sunflowers and the banner signify happiness, strength and growth. The huge sun shines brightly nourishing everything below.

The Sun card is a welcome card in any reading. There may be good news of a pregnancy, an engagement, a wedding or a celebration that brings friends and family together.

The Sun indicates a happy time for family matters, particularly if you have children, whatever their ages. This card can indicate that their lives may be about to change for the better. Family life will flow, and any recent dramas will be resolved. Negative issues of old will fade into the distant past.

The Sun card can literally mean sunshine, so maybe you have plans to travel somewhere hot. Planning a holiday is recommended, as is making plans for the future. Anything feels attainable now. You have an air of confidence about you, and your energy levels are high. If you are looking to start a new project, this is the perfect time to set things in motion. Opportunities will fall into place with little effort, and ideas and creativity will flow.

If you have just experienced a rough patch, then this is the card of breakthrough. At long last, your hard work and efforts are paying off. When the Sun card appears in a reading, everything is on its way to becoming brighter. The Sun's healing rays relate to good health and if there have been any concerns about health issues, either for you or a family member, then the outlook is good. This card suggests either the issue has been dealt with or is under control.

When we are working with the Sun's influence, we can get carried away with its optimistic energy and may fail to look at all aspects when making a decision. It is important to remember that if we stay in the sun too long, it can be harmful. Enjoy the positive energy around you, but be mindful that too much of a good thing can have a negative effect.

Reversed: Sadness, lack of success

Affirmation: *'I welcome all new opportunities. Now it is my time to welcome happiness and harmony into my life.'*

XX Judgement

Key words: Breakthrough, transformation, faith

Image: The Archangel Gabriel blows his trumpet as naked men, women and children rise in glory. There is a feeling of release and all that has passed has now been dealt with. A new dawn is about to rise.

If you have recently been through a period of struggle and frustration, then things are about to change. Decisions are being made that will release you from previous errors or judgement. This is a card of breakthrough, though your journey to this point has not been easy.

The Archangel Gabriel is our protector and guardian. With his energy looking after you, you need not fear. Gabriel cuts through illusions and allows us to see clearly what we need to be aware of. Although the journey to the Judgement card can be stressful, the outcome is one of huge relief.

If you feel that you are being judged, maybe now is the time to confront the perpetrators, there may have been a misunderstanding, which needs to be put right. Of course, it may be that you are the one being judgmental. If this is the case, be aware that we do not necessarily know other people's circumstances, even if we think we do. Whatever the reasons, there is no room in your life for this now, you have a more important journey to begin.

If you are carrying guilt, you must find a way to release it and let it go. A new phase is waiting for you, but it cannot begin until you deal with what is holding you back. You may have been dwelling on a situation and your mind may have been in turmoil, but what is done is done. Judgement is here not to judge you, but to set you free. It is important to understand that any decisions you made in the past, but now regret, were the right actions to take at that moment. If things did not go the way you planned, let this go now, as the universe has a different plan for you.

This card suggests you are ready for a fresh start, ready to throw away the shackles that bind you and seek fulfilment for your highest good. The Judgement card represents a breakthrough, so work out what is stopping you from reaching your true potential and make life happen!

Reversed: Delay, disappointment

Affirmation: *'I am optimistic about my future. This is the time for me to be who I want to be.'*

XXI The World

Key words: Change, movement, completion

Image: A woman dances within a wreath symbolizing the world as a cycle that has been completed, with a new phase ready to begin. The four figures surrounding the wreath are the same as those on the Wheel of Fortune and represent the four elements of earth, air, fire and water.

The World signifies completion or, in some cases, going full circle. It feels like everything is finally coming together and the struggle is over – there is a sense of peace around you.

You are moving into a period in your life in which there is much to look forwards to, as loose ends begin to be tied up and new opportunities are waiting to present themselves to you. Do not to resist change, as this is a good and abundant period in your life. Trust and go with the flow.

The important thing now is to keep on top of things and not to let old habits creep back into your life. You are experiencing a feeling of elation and relief and may find it difficult to maintain the positive aspects of all you have achieved. That is because you are feeling on a high; it would be impossible to maintain this mood for an extended period of time. However, at this time, you will feel you can achieve anything.

During the last few years, you have gained much wisdom. Use this now for making the right decisions. It may be that you are helping other people discover the right path. You may find friends sharing their problems with you, as you offer wise counsel and they trust your advice.

The World can also signify movement and travel. If you have been planning to move home, this is a positive time for action. If you are planning a trip, this is the perfect opportunity. It may be that you are meeting new friends, some who are well travelled or from across the globe. Your sense of adventure is heightened, and you will feel like a taste of the high life. A little indulgence at this time is recommended; don't feel guilty for treating yourself. You deserve it.

It is difficult to do wrong when you are working with the energy of the World, so trust your instincts and make your dreams a reality. The world really is at your feet.

Reversed: Lack of vision

Affirmation: *'My life is changing. I embrace all opportunities to be the best I can be.'*

Chapter 2

Using the Major Arcana

Tarot is a great tool for personal development and guidance and can also be used to help others who may be at a crossroad in their lives. I must stress I am not suggesting for one minute that you are ready to do a reading for anyone, but pulling a card for a friend in need is another matter. In fact, working with someone else will help you to gain confidence with the cards. This will be discussed in detail when we merge the Major and Minor Arcana cards together later in this book.

Shuffling

Shuffling the cards is a very important part of the reading process. Before shuffling, hold the cards between your hands for a few seconds to tune in to their vibration and connect your energy with the cards, then ask the question, either out loud or in your head, that you are seeking an answer to. Think about the question as you shuffle the cards. It may sound strange, but you will instinctively know when to stop shuffling. Once you feel you have shuffled enough, stop and turn over the top card, face up.

Some readers like to split the cards once they have been shuffled, then choose the top card from a certain pile. Personally, I do not agree with this. If you have shuffled and stopped with the cards in a particular formation, then I believe that is because this is the right place for you.

If you are pulling a card for another person, first shuffle the cards to connect with the cards' energy, then hand the deck to the querent and ask them to shuffle until it feels right for them to stop. Then ask them to hand the cards back to you so that you can lay the top card face up.

Over the years, I have noticed that the shuffling technique of the querent tells a story even before a card has been laid and the reading begins. For example, if the shuffle is slow and clumsy, this often relates to dithering and poor decision-making. If they are fast and erratic, then it infers they do not weigh up the consequences of their actions and can rush headlong into situations. If the cards are flying all over the place, it suggests that their life may well be all over the place too, and there are probably many different issues that need to be confronted. Finally, if the shuffling is calm and even, then they are more likely to heed the advice of the reading by looking at all the options open to them.

Tarot tip

As a beginner, start with all the cards in an upright position. This way, you will avoid reverse meanings until you feel confident.

Tarot reversals

I always recommend that beginners work with the cards in an upright position. However, reversed cards can play a part within a reading and, as you grow more familiar with the cards, that aspect will become clear. The reversed meaning is not necessarily the exact opposite of the upright meaning. It can be, but it can also simply lessen the intensity of the main meaning. It is important with a reversed card to read the upside-down image exactly as you feel and see it. Some people believe that reversed meanings are negative, but this is not the case. For example, the Tower card, which represents dramatic change and destruction, means in the reversed position that any changes ahead that might be a concern will not have a negative impact. Don't be afraid of reversed card meanings – allow your intuition to guide you.

Asking a question using one-card guidance

A great way of becoming familiar with the cards is to pull a Major Arcana card daily for guidance. At the end of the evening, you can compare your day with the meaning of the card; personal experience will help you to connect to the energy of the card quickly.

How you phrase a question can be the difference between receiving clear guidance or a garbled answer. There may be times when you turn a card that you feel does not answer the question at all. Questions should be to the point and not contain multiple options.

It is important that you ask a closed question. 'Will I get a new job?' is an open question, but 'Will I get a new job within the next six months?' is a closed and more specific question. Of course, sometimes it may be necessary to ask an open question. Just be aware that the answer you receive will be directly related to how you asked the question.

Let's assume that you have asked the question about changing jobs, you shuffle the cards and then turn over the Death card. As we have already discovered (*see page 43*), this relates to endings and beginnings so it is likely you will change your job. However, it is still the Death card, so it may imply the parting of ways will not be amicable. If, with the same question, you turn over the Hanged Man, it suggests that the timescale may be longer than six months as the Hanged Man holds you in suspension. Finally, asking the same question and turning over The Star, which is a card of new beginnings and letting go of the old, the answer will be a clear yes, and the change will come within the timescale you have requested.

Remember, don't panic if you pull the Tower or the Death card for guidance. The likely outcome is that you will be letting go of a situation.

Now you get the picture, let's ask more questions.

Question: Will I meet my soulmate this year?

The Devil: You have not fully released yourself from the emotional attachment of a previous relationship, and that is unconsciously blocking you from moving forwards.

The Lovers: It is very likely, so make sure you get out and about socially, and put yourself in situations where you will meet new people.

The Fool: It is possible you will meet someone soon. However, he or she is unlikely to be your soulmate, and you are more likely to have a fling or a short affair.

Question: Will my finances improve within the next year?

The Magician: Opportunities are around, but you are just not seeing the options. Look outside of your comfort zone to find your answers.

Death: You need to look closely at your financial situation and make major changes to your relationship with money. Take the time to study your bank statement. What is no longer needed? Are you getting the best deals? Are you in denial about how serious your financial situation is? Death suggests there are financial commitments you can let go of. Start today. It may not be easy, but small steps will have a huge impact on getting you out of the red and into the black.

Justice: You are struggling with your finances, possibly borrowing from Peter to pay Paul each month. This card suggests you need to bring balance into your financial situation, but unlike the Death card, it suggests that making your finances flow more easily should not take too much effort. You have the resources you need; you just have to make them work for you.

Question: Will my health improve?

The Star: An optimistic card of hope and opportunity. It suggests that whatever health issues are concerning you, this is just a passing phase of illness and there is nothing to worry about in the long term. The Star can help us to let go of old habits and become more aware of looking after our body. This may involve starting a healthy diet, exercising more, giving up smoking or alcohol, or anything that will help you to improve your lifestyle.

The Hanged Man: You may feel that you are not improving and find yourself frustrated with doctors' advice. Although this is not a negative card, it does suggest you are in limbo. If you are concerned about health issues and feel you have been pushed from pillar to post, maybe you need to request a further consultation so that you are clear about what to expect, and what positive action you can take to help yourself on the road to recovery.

Death: I have included the Death card with a health question, as it would not be unreasonable as a beginner at Tarot to fear the worst. The Death card suggests that there may have been a prolonged illness. This is a card of emotional upheaval and it indicates good and bad days. On a positive note, the Death card can signify a change in a situation as quickly as it developed, therefore allowing the healing process to start. The negative side of this card can suggest a life-changing illness – the death of life as you know it – but don't be disheartened by this interpretation. Millions of people live with controlled health issues and have a full and happy life.

Question: Will I find a job or a new career this year?

The High Priestess: As an intuitive card, it suggests you may have been searching half-heartedly for a new job or change in your career, applying too much thinking and not enough action. The High Priestess asks that you reconnect with your inner self. Ask for guidance, and listen. If you have a particular path you would like to follow but do not feel qualified or confident, then ask how you should move forwards in achieving your goals.

Strength: You may need to try harder and look at every option of finding your dream role. You have the Strength to do this, but it may be that you are not putting in enough effort. Be brave and bold, you have nothing to lose and everything to gain. Let the confident side of your personality shine – prospective employers will see this, too.

The Wheel of Fortune: Maybe you should be seeking a career far beyond what you believe is possible, one that has great prospects and offers the opportunity to earn a fabulous income. The Wheel of Fortune is about to turn for you and everything is ready to move forwards. Don't waste time thinking too much. This is a card of action and you need to get the wheel moving now.

Three-card readings

A basic three-card spread using the Major Arcana can give you a quick snapshot of a situation; it can also be used for a general reading. In other words, you do not have to focus on a specific question. Just shuffle and lay three cards face up from left to right and see what message they are presenting to you.

1. Past   2. Present   3. Future

A three-card spread is an easy way for you to begin to link cards together. As you become a more experienced Tarot reader, the greater the flow will become, enabling you to connect one card to the next.

To begin, I suggest you lay three cards with a specific question in mind and before you start to read, just take a minute to look at which cards have appeared before you.

It may be that as soon as the cards are laid, you can clearly see an obvious answer to your question. However, they may appear not to make any sense at all, nor connect to your question. If this happens, it is important to bear in mind, that although Tarot is a fantastic tool for guidance, sometimes we can ask questions that we are just not meant to know the answer to. Maybe this is a karmic situation and you have to consider decisions that could change the course of your current path. Should this happen, try rephrasing your question. The answer may not need to be direct at this time and the outcome of the spread may offer guidance rather than a yes or no answer.

Tarot tip

It is wise to make a note of the cards and in a few days revisit the original reading to see if the message has become clearer.

Historically, the three-card spread links to our past, present and future. When we interpret the past card, it can relate to just days or weeks before; it does not necessarily apply to the distant past (although this can happen if it is relevant to your question).

Examples of client readings using a three-card Major Arcana spread:

Cathy's Question: Will my new business succeed?

1. **Past – The Devil (enslavement):** Having to make personal sacrifices in the past had stopped her pursuing her dream. Commitments to family and her 'safe' job had taken priority, and she had not been in a position to have the freedom or luxury of branching out on her own.

2. **Present – The World (change):** With her children having left home, she no longer has the financial pressure to continue to commit to a job she loathes; it is time for her to embrace new prospects. The World suggests an exciting opportunity, and a chance to become financially independent in her own right.

3. **Future – The Empress (creativity):** Cathy has many hidden talents, and I feel she has all the tools she needs to make her business a success.

Richard's Question: Will I move abroad?

1. **Past – The Chariot (direction):** I could see that life had not been easy for Richard in recent years. He had been through many struggles and changes that he had been unable to control.

2. **Present – the Star (hope):** The opportunity of moving abroad and starting a new life was tempting, but maybe he was only seeing what he wanted through rose-tinted glasses. The Star represents pouring away the old to welcome in the new. However, what is around the corner is not necessarily better.

3. **Future – The Devil (enslavement):** I felt that now was not a good time to make such a major decision as he may well be jumping out of the frying pan and into the fire. The Devil entices us with temptation, and in the 'future' position warns that this is not a good time to make a dramatic move. Richard needs to look seriously at his options before making his final decision.

Linda's Question: Will my lover come back to me?

1. **Past – The Moon (deceit):** I felt there was another person involved and that her lover had been unfaithful to her. There had been issues in the relationship for some time, and she had ignored her intuition and not felt able to confront him.

2. **Present – The Fool (choice):** Who had been foolish? Linda's lover for deceiving her, or Linda for not trusting what she knew? Both were on a new path, but I felt that they were unhappy with their current situations. Her lover was regretting his actions, and his new relationship was likely doomed.

3. **Future – Temperance (patience):** I felt that they needed to rebuild trust and discuss why and how the relationship had broken down. Even though Linda was heartbroken and angry, she would find the strength to get through this. If they mutually agreed to try again, which I felt was likely, they would be able to clear the air and in time build a stronger bond than they had before.

Chapter 3

Which Major Arcana Card Are You?

Your Tarot birth card is calculated by adding up your birthday and reducing it down to its lowest denomination. We have been working with the Major Arcana cards, and this simple exercise will help you to discover who you are and why you may encounter certain patterns, habits and challenges throughout your life. Recognizing who you are in Tarot will help you to find the positive energies within the cards and use them to help balance your life.

Some people may have two birth cards, one dominant and the other a lesser energy from a supporting card, and I will explain this through examples as we go along.

Working out your Tarot birth card

Add the digits of your full birth date together.

For example, someone born on the 21 April 1988 would be 21/4/1988

Add the numbers together: 2+1+4+1+9+8+8 = 33

As the Major Arcana only goes up to 21, you will need to reduce this number down to its lowest denomination. To do that, you add those two numbers together.

Therefore 33 would be 3 +3 = 6

Your birth card number is 6.

6 = The Lovers

Those born under the Lovers' energies are caring and sensitive souls. This vibration relates to someone whose family and friends play a vital role in their lives – the home and having roots are extremely important. As a 'Lovers' child, when your time comes to have your own family, you will make a wonderful parent. You may even be a bit overprotective and sensitive to their needs. Your intuition and instinct make you want to rush around and do everything you can for those you care about, and you may become distracted from keeping your own life manageable. Don't forget to take care of yourself. You possess a deep intuition about those close to you and will not stand by and let injustice happen.

More examples of Birth Card numbers and what they mean

Date of birth: 23 March 1952 = 23/3/1952

Add the numbers together: 2+3+3+1+9+5+2 = 25

Add those numbers together to get a number between 1–21 (the Major Arcana numbers)

2+5 = 7

7 = The Chariot

The Chariot relates to balance, control and energy. Being born under this vibration does in itself bring a path of choices and challenges, some not always easy to resolve. However, the Chariot is always the victor, even if it sometimes feels like it has taken forever to reach your desired goal. You will get there in the end.

You may be a bit of a ditherer when deciding your own fate and have a tendency of putting others before your own needs. You may know what you have to do but feel that you do not have the strength to put the plans into action. As your confidence grows, so will your positive attitude and this will help you to make things happen. Under this influence, you are able to overcome all obstacles and resistance. When you feel that the odds are against you, be comforted by the fact that your destiny is clear. You will find your path and follow it.

Date of birth: 9 June 1965 = 9/6/1965

Add the numbers together: = 9+6+1+9+6+5 = 36

Add those numbers together to get a number between 1 and 21 (the Major Arcana numbers) 3+6 = 9

9 = The Hermit

The Hermit has a quiet air and although this implies you are happy with your own company, the challenge is to be more adventurous and not afraid to step outside your comfort zone. This vibration is studious and spiritual. You will never be happy with 'half-cocked' answers – there is a need to look deep inside to find out answers for yourself. The Hermit continually searches for the 'right' path, and those born under this vibration may encounter many twists and turns throughout their lives. To make long-term plans, sometimes you have to look back before you can move forwards, examining the patterns of behaviour of both yourself and those close to you to see how they have required you to make decisions somewhere along the line. You will have an interest in psychic and spiritual matters, but often under this vibration may lack the confidence to allow your light to shine. You could be a wonderful healer and a gifted psychic.

Examples of people with two birth cards

If the sum of birth date numbers is a double-digit figure that can be reduced down again to a number below 21, then the person with that birth date has two birth cards: a dominant one, and a lesser energy (supporting) one.

Date of birth: 10 July 1964 = 10/7/1964

Add the numbers together: 1+0+7+1+9+6+4 = 28; 2+8 = 10

10 is a double digit number that when added together totals less than 21, so this birth date has two birth cards – 10 and 1+0 = 1 (therefore creating a major and lesser/supporting card)

10 and 1 = Wheel of Fortune/The Magician

10/1 = Wheel of Fortune/The Magician

The Magician holds all the tools he/she needs to be versatile and to put plans into action. This energy is complemented by the Wheel of Fortune, which offers you many opportunities, sometimes through luck and chance. You will have a natural skill of turning thoughts into reality.

This is an ambitious combination, and anyone born under these influences will achieve many goals throughout their lifetime. The Wheel is constantly turning, and of course there will be both highs and lows. However, with the Magician as a secondary energy, you are a quick thinker and have the tools to get out of sticky situations. You are likely to be impatient when things are not flowing as they should, but learn to trust your intuition on a daily basis and you will find life much calmer!

You can sometimes be a bit hard on yourself, as these cards suggest you can be a perfectionist. You may have a lot of projects on the go and need to prioritize what needs completing first. You are creative and 'psychic' and have a deep interest in anything esoteric (teaching Tarot is a perfect job for you!). The Wheel could suggest issues with finances and needing to get tighter control over your monthly income and expenditure. A powerful combination, be imaginative in your dreams as these cards are full of movement, activity and the ability to succeed!

Date of birth: 5 November 1957 = 5/11/1957

Add the numbers together: 5+1+1+1+9+5+7 = 29

Add those numbers together 2+9 = 11

Because 11 is a double digit number that adds up to less than 21, we have a secondary birth card 11 (1+1 = 2) so the birth cards are 11 and 2.

11 and 2 = Justice/The High Priestess

11/2 = Justice/The High Priestess

If these two cards influence your path, you will most certainly be interested in psychic and spiritual matters! You may find it difficult to compromise, as you can be a perfectionist. There is a focused sense of reaching your goals, and you will work as hard as is required to achieve the results you seek. Your numbers generally show a sense of individualism, maybe working best when you are alone in your creative state of mind. You have deep, imaginative thoughts, and are highly 'sensitive' to your surroundings and people. Trusting your intuition is not a problem, but Justice brings the need to question your choices to ensure you have made the correct decisions. If something is not right, you may lose interest quickly rather than battle through until the end. Embrace the great intuitive qualities of the High Priestess, don't allow yourself to walk a path you do not choose or enjoy. Justice demands everything be truthful, strong, balanced and fair. Accept only what is right for you and your destiny will be clear.

Before we leave the Birth cards, here is a quick guide to help you with their meanings.

Birth card meanings at a glance		
0	The Fool	Likes to take risks, enjoys change but must not confuse being reckless with being adventurous
1	The Magician	Adaptable, hard-working and capable
2	The High Priestess	Intuitive, counsellor, wise beyond years
3	The Empress	Motherly, protective, a worrier
4	The Emperor	Controlled, disciplined and ambitious
5	The Hierophant	Spiritual, likes to plan and be part of a community
6	The Lovers	Caring person, can be overly sensitive, family orientated
7	The Chariot	Hardworking and resourceful. Indecisive, can find it hard to put roots down
8	Strength	A solid and trusted friend, dependable and reliable, takes on challenges and responsibility, often emotional
9	The Hermit	A spiritual person, a deep thinker who enjoys solitude
10	Wheel of Fortune	Enjoys the finer things in life, needs to be aware of the negative and positive energy of money
11	Justice	Logical and honest, harmony and balance are important, but can be challenging
12	The Hanged Man	Too much thinking and not enough action, can be a martyr, may be indecisive but often sees both sides of a disagreement; a great mediator
13	Death	Periods of dramatic and sudden changes; expect the unexpected
14	Temperance	Patient and caring, a natural healer
15	The Devil	Responsible, a tendency to be controlled by others, must learn to trust own strengths
16	The Tower	The ability to learn from past mistakes, bounces back from challenging situations
17	The Star	Optimistic outlook on life, a very blessed birth card
18	The Moon	Very psychic, must learn to control their emotions in a positive way
19	The Sun	Dedicated to creating family harmony, a devoted friend
20	Judgement	Stumbling blocks and breakthroughs
21	The World	A wise visionary; loves to travel, complete projects and go full circle

Working out your year card

Expanding on your birth card, you can also work out what card will influence your year ahead. Your year card does not begin on the 1st January but on your birthday and will play a major part in your year going forwards.

To work out your year card, take your birthday excluding the year you were born. Replace the year you were born with the year you are approaching.

For example, if your birthday is the 15 June, add 15 and 6 plus the year approaching. If the year approaching is 2014 the numbers would be 15/6/2014.

Therefore, you would add 1 + 5 + 6 + 2 + 0 + 1 + 4 = 19 (19 = The Sun)

Then as with the birth cards, you would add 1 + 9 = 10 to find the lesser energy or supporting card.

10 = Wheel of Fortune. So, your cards for the upcoming year would be the Sun and the Wheel of Fortune. What a fabulous combination that is! Then, using your Tarot skills learned in the previous chapters, work out what your year card means to you.

If you calculate your year card and it is Death or the Tower, don't panic. Just be aware it may be a year of changes and challenges. The lesser card will help you to face any difficulties with strength.

Helpful card calculations

If you want to choose a date for a particular event, you can use the Major Arcana cards to help calculate and guide you. For example, if you are planning a wedding, add up your proposed dates using this system and choose the date and card that inspires you. If you have a job interview, this can be a helpful method to steer the interview to your advantage.

For instance, a friend of mine went for an interview on the 1st April 2014.

1+4+2+0+1+4 = 12, 12 = The Hanged Man.

I felt they would not rush to give him an answer. He would definitely be in the running but there was someone else with equal qualifications. In other words, the decision would be held in suspension. If he did not get a positive response quickly, then he would not get the job. They promised they would be in touch by the end of the week, but three weeks passed, and they then said no; it was very close between him and one other candidate. If we had worked out the date and card before the interview, I would have told him to be more dynamic and aggressive to stand out from the crowd. The Hanged Man can be disruptive, and if pulled under certain circumstances, you may need to have your wits about you.

With a bit of preparation and knowledge of the card energy, you can turn a situation to your advantage with little effort.

Before we leave the Major Arcana, here is a quick guide to help you narrow down the time scale of a predicted outcome.

Major Arcana cards and timescales		
0	The Fool	No season
I	The Magician	Spring
II	The High Priestess	Autumn
III	The Empress	Summer
IV	The Emperor	Summer
V	The Hierophant	Autumn
VI	The Lovers	Spring
VII	The Chariot	Summer
VIII	Strength	Winter
IX	The Hermit	Winter
X	Wheel of Fortune	All seasons
XI	Justice	Winter
XII	The Hanged Man	Autumn
XIII	Death	Winter
XIV	Temperance	Spring
XV	The Devil	Autumn
XVI	The Tower	Winter
XVII	The Star	Spring
XVIII	The Moon	Spring
XIX	The Sun	Summer
XX	Judgement	Winter
XXI	The World	Summer

Tarot tip

Another great way to learn the deeper meanings of the cards is by meditating and doing creative visualization exercises with them.

Wheel of Fortune meditation

Close your eyes and imagine you are in a large open park. In the distance, you see an old-fashioned Ferris wheel standing alone; there is no one around, just you. There is one open carriage on the Ferris wheel and you walk towards it. You step inside the carriage and close the door. You sit on a wooden seat and see a small table opposite you. As you look above and around the carriage, you notice it is decorated with a huge collage of Tarot cards. There are hundreds of cards scattered over the walls and ceiling. The colours fascinate you, and many of the pictures are from decks you have never seen before.

The wheel begins to turn and as it ascends, a card drops to your feet. This is the card of your desires. Look at it. What is its message? What do you need right now? You place the card on the table before you, and the wheel continues to turn upwards.

Another card falls by your feet. Again, you pick it up. This is the card of your fears. Look at the card in detail, the message shows you what you need to work on. Lay this card on the table next to the first one. The wheel continues to turn, until it reaches the top, and then another card drops to your feet. Pick it up, this is the card of how you can conquer your fears, the guidance you need right now to let go. Lay the card on the table.

Now the wheel begins to descend, and another card flutters down to. This is the card of your truth: what are you avoiding? This message will guide you to see things more clearly. The wheel continues to descend, as yet another card drops at your feet. This time it is a card you do not recognize, the symbols, pictures and colours are unique and this card only has meaning to you. Its role is to give you clarity within a situation. Ask now for direction. When you have finished, lay the card at the end of the row and look at this reading with fresh eyes. What is it telling you? What is your message?

The Ferris wheel comes to a halt, and for a moment you reflect on your journey. The message of the Wheel reminds us that we should not simply stand still and accept what life hands us. We have the choice and free will to take action to change what needs to be changed. Do not be fearful. Now you have finished your journey, leave the cards on the table and step out of the carriage. You feel lighter, calmer and ready to work with the guidance from your reading.

Part II

THE MINOR ARCANA

The Minor Arcana comprises 56 cards from four suits – Pentacles, Swords, Wands and Cups – and represents the practical issues of everyday life.

Chapter 4

Cards of the Minor Arcana

The Minor Arcana is comprised of 56 cards which, with the Major Arcana, complete the traditional Tarot deck of 78 cards. The Minor Arcana is also referred to as the lesser Arcana, and the cards as the pip cards, as they relate to the more mundane aspects of daily life.

As we have already noted, the Minor Arcana consists of four suits: Pentacles, Swords, Wands and Cups, also known as Coins, Swords, Batons and Cups depending on the deck you are using.

Each suit has 14 cards, consisting of 10 numbered cards and four Court cards – Page, Knight, Queen and King. We will work with the Court cards in Chapter 6. Each suit is associated with one of the elements: earth, air, fire or water.

Pentacles (Coins) relate to the element of earth (physical) and represent earthly matters such as, money, security, the home and other material aspects.

Swords relate to the element of air (thought) and represent our thoughts, daydreams, ideas, conflicts and strife.

Wands (Batons) relate to the element of fire (spirit) and are associated with ambition, drive and energy. Wands also connect to work and making change happen.

Cups relate to the element of water (emotion) and represent emotional issues such as our love life, family, emotional behaviour and how we deal with relationships.

A perfect reading would have a balance of the four suits with one or two Major Arcana cards included in the spread. However, this seldom happens as readings tend to be dominated by specific issues. For example, if Pentacles dominate a reading, it indicates that the situation is too grounded and there is no flexibility enabling the querent to find alternative solutions. If Swords dominate a reading, it signifies that there is too much thinking and not enough action. If Wands dominate a reading, there is too much energy being focused in the wrong area, and finally, if Cups dominate a reading, then you are allowing your emotions to cloud your judgement.

Tarot tip

If a suit is absent in a reading, it signifies a lack of that particular energy. This needs to be addressed so that balance can be restored.

The suit of Pentacles (earth)

Ace of Pentacles

Key words: Opportunity, money, new beginnings

Image: The Ace of Pentacles shows a hand emerging from a cloud, below which there is an abundant garden full of trees bearing fruit.

This is a positive card that represents a new opportunity or a gift of money. It reminds us that our fate is in our hands and that we have the power to create abundance in any circumstances. If your finances are in a dire state, the Ace of Pentacles sends a positive message that things can quickly change for the better if you look seriously at ways of removing any obstacles. If you are looking for work or starting a business, this is a very good time to get the ball rolling and plant the seeds of new ideas.

Although we often associate this card with money, it can also relate to juggling home life, health issues and work. This is a practical card and will bring stability to the area of your life that is currently causing you concern. Under the influence of this card, you will find a little extra effort will go a long way.

Reversed: Materialism and worry

Two of Pentacles

Key words: Balance, instability, juggling situations

Image: A young man juggles two coins within the tilted figure 8 (the symbol of infinity), while in the background two sailing ships battle rocky seas.

This card suggests you are juggling too many things and need to create balance. It is likely that your finances are an issue and you are looking for ways to get out of the red and into the black. Closely examining your spending habits might be a good idea now. However, be comforted by the knowledge that your financial problems can be resolved with a little effort. Change is often around the corner with the Two of Pentacles.

You may feel overburdened by too many demands on your time and finances, resulting in a feeling that you are on an emotional roller coaster. There may be occasions when you are so overwhelmed with mundane everyday tasks that you have no time for what is important. Look carefully at the issues that are currently draining your time, energy and resources. Prioritize what is important right now.

Reversed: Difficulties, money worries

Three of Pentacles

Key words: Hard work, appreciation

Image: A young man works in a cathedral, watched by two architects who discuss the plans while admiring his skills.

If you feel you are unappreciated in your workplace, be reassured your dedication and job skills are not going unnoticed. Still, you may feel you are not being adequately financially rewarded for all you do, especially considering the time and energy expended beyond the call of duty. It may be you do not delegate enough, believing that if you do it yourself, it will get done properly and more quickly. You work hard and are a natural team leader. However, by assuming much of the responsibility, you place too much pressure on yourself.

This card shows you have the ability, knowledge and competence beyond the skills required for the job in hand. Maybe it is time to look at a more ambitious challenge where your skills will be more appreciated. You are diligent and able to perfect all you need to, down to the smallest detail. You are able to work to deadlines even if it means pushing yourself to the limit.

Reversed: Incompetence, neglect

Four of Pentacles

Key words: Meanness, short-sightedness, hoarding

Image: A man sits on a bench surrounded by four coins: he is holding a coin, balancing one on his head, and there is one under each foot.

This card represents holding on to your finances or being over-possessive, and although it usually relates to material issues, it can also represent holding on to your emotions, or bottling up your thoughts. It can denote a controlling nature or someone who is not willing to share. Pulling this card indicates that now is not the time to confide secrets or ideas in anyone less than trustworthy.

To the outside world you may appear to hold your cards close to your chest, perhaps occasionally appearing mean and ungenerous. Maybe it is time to loosen the purse strings and show another side to your nature. Of course, there are times in life when it's necessary to keep money and ideas close to home, but it's always advisable to get the balance right.

This card encourages you to be prudent with finances and, if possible, save a little each month, particularly if you have experienced hardship in the past. It is time to change your attitude towards money; give and you shall receive.

Reverse: Obstacles, extravagance, spendthrift

Five of Pentacles

Key words: Overwhelmed by worry, hardship, feeling abandoned

Image: Two beggars walk barefoot in the snow. Above them is the beautiful stained glass window of a church, but one of the beggars only looks down and does not see the beauty above him.

This card can represent a period of hardship, a feeling of despair. You may have been in a negative situation for a while and cannot see an answer to your problems. This card urges you to look beyond your current difficulties, whether they are of a financial or emotional nature. Often, when we are overwhelmed with worry, we do not see that we are blessed with a home, friends, and food on the table.

This card asks us to look at what is important and reminds us not to feel sorry for ourselves.

If you have been feeling tired and lethargic, the Five of Pentacles can reflect health issues so ensure you are not neglecting your own needs. If you have any concerns about your health, now is the time to seek medical advice, although it is probable you are worrying over nothing, it will give you peace of mind.

Reversed: New opportunities, money issues being resolved

Six of Pentacles

Key words: Giving, inequality, sharing

Image: A man holding aloft a set of scales in his left hand representing balance and imbalance, stands over two beggars who are kneeling at his feet. He gives money to one while neglecting the other who kneels with his hand outstretched.

It is time for you to look at your financial situation, as it seems there is a discrepancy between your incomings and your outgoings. As quickly as money comes in, out it goes again, and it is possible you are in denial about your financial situation. The situation is unlikely to be resolved unless you take control now. Drastic action needs to be taken with regard to your spending habits. If you have been helping someone financially, it is time they took back control of their own situation and remove the burden from you.

You are too generous for your own good, and it is time to say no to those who take advantage as your need is greater than theirs. This card can also relate to someone close to you, perhaps a partner, a family member or your employer. A feeling of being undervalued often surfaces with this card. It is also possible that someone around you is controlling the finances to the point where you are finding it difficult to keep your head above water.

Reversed: Unfairness, jealousy, bribery

Seven of Pentacles

Key words: Reward, growth, achievement

Image: A man with a self-satisfied expression enjoys a break from work, leaning on his spade while gazing at a crop of coins before him.

This represents hard work and fruitful investments. It is a time of contemplation, and it may also be that you are on the verge of making major changes in your life. The card suggests that, financially, you are comfortable or you are about to make a decision that will increase your financial potential.

Nothing in life comes easily, and you will have to invest your own hard work to benefit from the fruits of your labour. However, it seems you are entering a very fortunate phase now. There may have been past hardships, but you are about to venture onto a new path. If you are looking for a challenge, the time is right to plant the seeds for a new opportunity to grow and prosper. This is a card of success. Still, it requires your hard work to support any new ventures, as success will not be handed to you on a plate. However, if you are prepared to work hard, all you desire will be achieved.

Reversed: Bad investments, disappointment, lack of progress

Eight of Pentacles

Key words: Hard work, conscientious, creativity

Image: A young man sitting astride a bench appears to be completely focused on making coins. He is absorbed in getting the job done with accuracy and perfection.

This is a card of great potential. If you are feeling in a productive mood, focus on your goal and be ready to put in all the work and effort required to complete your task. Don't underestimate how hard you have worked to get to this point in your life. You are almost there and your attention to detail and clarity in what you are trying to achieve is heightened now. This card can represent a stressful period in your life, if you are working, you may be feeling particularly pressured at this time.

If you are looking for work or employment, then this card suggests a new opportunity is near. If you are considering starting your own business, this is a very good time to begin. You may also be looking to work from home and create space to dedicate to your work.

This card can suggest that you may require the additional skills of someone who is a master at their craft. If this is the case, you will not have to look too hard, as suitable people will gravitate towards you.

Reversed: Lack of drive and ambition, lazy

Nine of Pentacles

Key words: Accomplishment, material comfort

Image: An elegant woman with a small bird on her raised, gloved hand stands in front of a beautiful landscape. Her robes and surroundings appear luxurious, suggesting a decadent lifestyle.

It is likely you have come through the other side of a difficult period in your life and feel relaxed and hopeful about the future, although after experiencing a certain amount of drama and excitement, life may appear to be too quiet. The negative side of this card can be boredom. Have you reached a point in your life where you would like more adventure or a challenge? In some instances, this card can suggest a physical change such as a new hairstyle, revamping your wardrobe or beginning a healthier lifestyle or diet.

You have accomplished much but perhaps the spark has gone from your life. On the one hand, you may be fulfilled on a financial level but on the other feel the need for a new challenge. You decide to live your life on your own terms as you have gone through hardships in order to know your own mind and what is best for you. Remind yourself how hard you have worked to get to this point. Now is the time for rewards. You may be feeling extravagant, and if you can afford to indulge yourself, then why not!

Reversed: Loss, frivolity, bad investments

Ten of Pentacles

Key words: Fulfilment, wealth, abundance

Image: In a busy scene in a town square with people chatting, a child hides behind his mother's robe and a wise man looks on with an air of contentment as two dogs wait obediently by their master.

This is a card of material wealth, a reminder that all is well. It could be that you have come into money from an unexpected source such as an inheritance, a bonus, a new job, a promotion or a windfall. However this financial abundance has come to you, it is much appreciated, and life will now feel more solid and grounded. If you have been concerned about money issues, this will soon come to an end.

Family issues are prominent now, and you may be in a position to help someone out either financially or physically. You feel secure in your current state of affairs and, as you look at those close to you, they also appear to be in balance. This is a time when you can reflect on the past and be proud that you have achieved so much – it is time to enjoy all you have worked for.

Reversed: Misfortune, loss, failure

The suit of Swords (air)

Ace of Swords

Key words: Victory, breakthrough, clear vision

Image: A hand appears from a cloud holding an upright sword. At the tip of the sword is a crown with a wreath, symbolizing victory. The ground below is barren and mountainous.

Aces always represent the possibility of new beginnings. The message of the Ace of Swords is that ideas in the mind have the potential to become reality. It is time to cut through the illusion, as a breakthrough has happened or is about to happen. It is likely that you have been toying with ideas, chopping and changing your mind as to how to proceed. The Ace of Swords represents a light-bulb moment when everything is about to fall into place. As this is the first card of the suit, you will still be at the idea stage. However, it feels that your vision can become reality at last.

Swords represent conflict and strife, so ensure that the plans concerning the forwards movement of any new projects are clear and concise. If others are involved it is important that everyone knows their role. If there are challenges ahead, make sure that you have all the resources you need to overcome any obstacles.

Reversed: Lack of focus, dominance, obstacles

Two of Swords

Key words: Stalemate, frustration, lack of options

Image: A woman sits on a stone seat in front of the sea, blindfolded so that she cannot see what the future holds. Her arms are crossed in front of her chest, and in each hand she holds a sword pointing upwards. The sea behind her is still, but there are treacherous-looking rocks in the distance.

This card tells us that we are seeing only what we choose to see. There are options; you are just not looking hard enough for solutions or maybe you don't want to take an alternative route. You may be in denial or are being stubborn over a situation, but something will have to give in order to move forwards. Your current indecision is causing you stress, and you may feel that you are being pulled in two directions.

Sometimes we just have to wait and let the issue concerning us calm down before we take action. The universe has its own way of stopping us in our tracks. Use this time to try to think clearly about what you truly want from life right now. Tune in to your intuition, as you have been so busy stressing over your situation that you are not listening to what it is telling you.

Reversed: Potential danger, awareness

Three of Swords

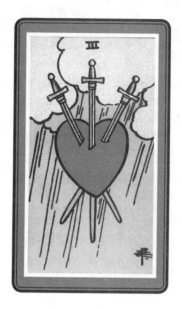

Key words: Sorrow, grief, heartache

Image: A large red heart has been pierced by three swords; the bleak grey background sums up the emotion of this card.

This is a card of sorrow and heartbreak relating to deep emotional issues. However, this card is not all doom and gloom as it can be associated with emotional issues of the past and, although the pain has gone, this might imply that you have not completely let go. Perhaps it relates to a relationship that has gone sour, but the pain is still with you. If this is the case, you need to find a way to deal with these emotions and heal them fully in order to move on. The very fact this card has turned up in a reading means you are holding on to old, negative emotions. If you are in a relationship, it is possible you are experiencing a difficult patch. This card is not a good omen for a successful outcome and therefore issues need to be addressed in order to progress. Symbolically, as we begin to remove each sword the healing process is able to commence. Be kind to yourself, as things will get better.

Reversed: Confusion, loss

Four of Swords

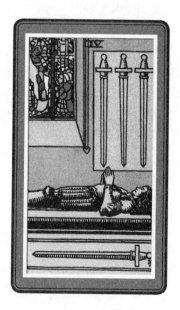

Key words: Meditation, rest, healing

Image: The figure of a Knight lies on a stone tomb; his hands clasped in prayer. Three swords are suspended above him, and one is embedded in the tomb. The sword that lies beneath him symbolizes an issue that is troubling the querent. Above him is a stained-glass window.

It is likely you have experienced a stressful period and need to rest and recuperate. It is important that you ground yourself before making any major changes. If you are able to do this, you will view the issue in a new and more positive light. If a stressful problem has been ongoing, try using a different tactic. Too much thinking and not enough action may play a part in prolonging the agony.

It is important that you take time to recharge your batteries. You may have been through months of challenges. It is now advisable to take time out to unwind so that you are ready for the positive changes that the future will bring.

This card is sometimes known as the card of meditation as, if you are able to meditate, you will reap huge benefits. However, if meditation is not for you, try just having some quiet time to reconnect with your inner wisdom.

Reversed: Restlessness, agitation, stress

Five of Swords

Key words: Conflict, strife, fighting

Image: A man holds three discarded swords as other men walk away from him. He has won the battle but at a price. Because the other men turn their backs on him, there is a sense of abandonment. The victory is hollow.

This card suggests that conflict, and challenges surround you. Keep calm and allow difficult issues to resolve themselves. Someone close to you may be looking for an argument but do not rise to the bait. Control your emotions, otherwise issues may escalate and get out of hand.

Whether you are facing mental or physical conflict, it may feel as if you are in the middle of a battle zone. Everywhere you turn, there is another issue waiting to be dealt with. Nothing is flowing or coming easily to you at this time. You may be battling with strong personalities and feel that you are compromising your integrity. Although you may be in a stubborn mood, you will have to consider a little more give and take if you wish to resolve issues quickly and without further conflict. If you are feeling like a victim in a situation, mediation will help to bring matters to a close.

Reversed: Unfairness, isolation, unhappy resolution

Six of Swords

Key words: Travel, emotional shifts, change

Image: A man steers a small boat with a woman and a child as passengers. Six swords stand prominently within the boat. The water to the left of the boat is calm signifying that you are sailing towards calmer waters. The water to the right is rough.

This card signifies that you have been through emotional turmoil but are now working towards a brighter future. However, this may not be as easy as it sounds. There is much to deal with, but most importantly you need to draw a line under an unpleasant situation in order for you to move forwards. You need to remind yourself that there is always a light at the end of the tunnel.

This card reminds us that we must not hold on to the negative influences of the past, as signified by the rocky waters to the right of the boat, which reflect the turbulent emotions you have experienced. You have the opportunity of a new beginning so do not allow grief, anger or resentment to weaken your resolve in making a better life.

This card can occasionally literally mean to sail across water. Maybe you are planning a trip? If this is the case, time away will be a healing experience for you despite whatever and whomever you have had to leave behind.

Reversed: Postponed journeys, stagnant energy

Seven of Swords

Key words: Deception, over-confident, thief

Image: A man holding five swords tiptoes away from a scene leaving behind two swords he is unable to carry. There is an air of smugness about him, as he appears to have got away with theft.

If you have a feeling that someone around you is not telling the whole truth, then you are probably right. You may have been drawn into a situation that makes you feel uncomfortable. If this is the case, you are advised to step away now, as it is possible you will become the scapegoat. If you feel you are moving aimlessly forwards without clear insight and direction, it's time to have your wits about you.

Open your eyes and trust your instincts with regards to other peoples' actions and motives.

This is a card of caution advising that you must no longer bury your head in the sand over a worrying situation. Now is the time to face the consequences. Avoiding the truth will only make matters worse and your fears are likely to be exposed. If others are offering advice do not let yourself be bullied into reacting to a situation that makes you uncomfortable. Allow yourself to be guided by your own intuition, as you will rarely be wrong.

Reversed: Revival, return of lost items

Eight of Swords

Key words: Restriction, confusion, trapped

Image: A woman who is tied and blindfolded stands helplessly surrounded by eight swords, which appear to imprison her. The town fades in the background, and she feels isolated and alone.

The blindfolded woman in this card has great significance as she represents your inability to believe you will ever be free of your current worries. Sometimes even the smallest of problems can seem overwhelming – whether you are burdened by an unhappy relationship, money worries or work-related issues, every problem has an answer. It is important to remember that you always have a choice. The choices you make may not be easy; in fact, it is likely you are facing tough challenges in resolving your difficulties. However, one small step forwards may be all that is needed to make a positive difference.

It is time to look at your options and you may indeed have to face your fears, but the situation may not be as bad as you believe. Nothing can make you feel as negative as you do right now. Look for the answers; they are there. You just have to put in the effort to begin your new journey.

Reversed: Freedom, power, new beginnings

Nine of Swords

Key words: Worry, sleepless nights, guilt

Image: The figure of a person (male or female) sits upright in bed with their head in their hands, consumed by worry and despair. Nine swords sit starkly against the background; the quilt is covered in astrological symbols.

At times, life appears to be overwhelming and dark thoughts can consume us as at any moment. I often refer to this card as the 3 a.m. card. Swords represent overthinking, and the Nine of Swords is probably the most significant indicator of this. You may find yourself dwelling on the negative rather than looking for the positive solutions. Perhaps you are so overwhelmed by despair that you can't see there is a light at the end of the tunnel. Too much thinking and not enough action; no wonder you are not sleeping.

There can be a sense of being consumed by guilt with this card but whatever happened in the past, you reacted in the way that you believed was right for you at the time. There is no place in our lives for guilt, as what is done is done. So move on! You may feel low, perhaps even depressed at the moment, but it will pass. Everyone experiences a Nine-of-Swords moment in life from time to time, but we use this time to learn and grow.

Reversed: Healing, good news, additional options

Ten of Swords

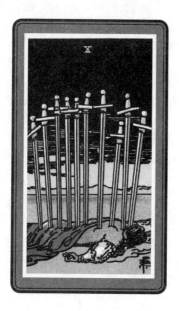

Key words: Victim, self-pity, sacrifice

Image: A victim lies face down on the ground with ten swords impaled in his back. The sea in the background is calm indicating that the negative aspect, which was quick and painful, has passed. The picture in this card is often more dramatic than the current situation.

Perhaps you have been emotionally stabbed in the back, or been a victim of someone's wrath. As a number 10 card and therefore the last number of the suit, this appears as a reminder that endings and beginnings are a natural part of the cycle of life. Move on. Whoever you have had an issue with, it is now time to let it go.

There is a possibility that you have been doing too much for others without any thanks or appreciation, or you are feeling burdened by an ongoing commitment. It is time to consider whether you are prepared to give generously or not at all, as the pressure is getting to you. What started as a helping hand now makes you feel resentful. Remove yourself from this situation though be aware you may end up being the 'bad guy'. Be cautious how you approach the situation, but release the burden and pressures that are holding you back.

Reversed: Trust, balance, healthy attitude

The suit of Wands (fire)

Ace of Wands

Key words: Ambition, inspiration, power

Image: A hand, holding aloft a wand with both buds and old leaves shedding, emerges through a cloud. Below is a landscape of mountains, water, trees and a castle, which represent opportunities.

The Ace of Wands brings with it new beginnings and vibrant energy, so all you are required to do is step outside of your comfort zone and go for it. If you have begun a new project or business, you are now laying the foundations for a fruitful future.

We often have a light-bulb moment with this card, as it is a clear indication of a time of opportunities. There is an enthusiastic energy about you, and you are ready for a challenge, raring to go. So, it is now time to make changes for the better. Although this is an extremely positive card, if you are starting a new project, you must still be cautious in your approach as, in your enthusiasm, you may overlook important issues.

Do not waste time thinking too much, because this is a card that requires action. Your time is now. Begin planning how you intend to move forwards and make the changes you need – things will move quickly once you open the floodgates!

Reversed: Setbacks, disappointment, delay

Two of Wands

Key words: Adventure, change, planning

Image: A man, holding a globe symbolizing the world is his oyster, stands between two wands. The diverse scene around him of the sea, the mountains and a green landscape indicates every direction offers a different opportunity.

This card suggests you have a new-found confidence and it is likely you have experienced, or are about to experience, a successful period in your life. Luck is on your side with this card. Gambles pay off and opportunities can present themselves to you without much effort on your part. You are about to walk a new path, so think carefully about your choices. Whatever path you choose, be aware that you are in control of your destiny.

This is an ambitious card, and if you feel you are at a crossroads now is the time to plan how you will make changes happen. The Two of Wands reminds you that your destiny is in your hands, and you may be feeling courageous enough to conquer the world. You may be planning a physical change, a house move or a new job but whatever it is, your life is about to take a new path.

Reversed: Caution, restriction, powerlessness

Three of Wands

Key words: Adventure, planning ahead, leadership

Image: A man stands looking out at the horizon surrounded by three wands. Although the landscape looks bleak, he knows it is a big, wide world out there, full of opportunity.

This card represents vision and looking to the future. It is time to consider your options, but don't necessarily take the first opportunity that comes to you. Take time to think about your current situation as, whatever you decide to do now, will affect your long-term future. You may be feeling confident and able to control what happens around you. It is a time for looking at greater possibilities. You are being encouraged to dream beyond your current limitations.

This card also represents adventure, a desire for a change of scenery and discovery. You may find yourself dreaming about visiting faraway places and there is no reason why this should not become a reality. If you are planning a group activity, you will be taking a leading role in making this happen. You may also be thinking about moving home or changing your job and there is a sense of having 'itchy feet'. You are ready for new challenges and the only person stopping you is you!

Reversed: Errors, insecurity, lack of vision

Four of Wands

Key words: Celebration, harmony, home

Image: Four wands support a wreath of flowers, beneath which are two people who are dancing in celebration. Behind them is a castle where a gathering has taken place.

This is a joyful card and it can relate to happy family gatherings, possibly news of a marriage, an anniversary or a birthday, any occasion when family and friends come together in celebration. This is one of the most positive cards in the Tarot deck and it often appears after a time of challenges. It signifies that you are now entering a new and happy phase in your life and have much to look forwards to, including achieving your goals. If you have been working on a project, you are now nearing completion and about to enter a new phase. We do not always know what will change the course of our life to make it more balanced and joyful, but the Four of Wands prepares us for what is about to happen. If you have been in an unhappy situation, you will soon find the strength to change things. This is a card that is full of surprises. Expect the unexpected in a positive way, as your life is about to take a turn for the better.

Reversed: Disputes, unwelcome change

Five of Wands

Key words: Conflict, tension, challenges

Image: Five men are brandishing wands and appear to be in battle. But look more closely – they are not striking each other, and no one is being harmed. This is a struggle for power rather than a physical challenge.

This card indicates a volatile situation, disagreements and quarrels often just for the sake of being argumentative. It is unlikely you are able to resolve conflict at present. There may be disharmony, either within the workplace or closer to home. As a fire card, it is fuelled by a lack of understanding, whether on your part or that of another person. The inability to be able to smooth out disagreements is frustrating, but this may be because you feel so strongly about your own views. However, a little give and take is needed if this is to be resolved.

Work issues may have been a bit of a battleground recently, and you may have to defend your actions or work harder than ever to prove yourself. This card can also represent an inner conflict. Take a deep breath before making decisions, as you need to calm your mind. Any frustration you are experiencing will pass, but you will have to find a compromise within yourself or with others before harmony is restored.

Reversed: Competition, assumptions, frustration

Six of Wands

Key words: Success, journey, triumph

Image: A man on horseback holds a wand bearing a wreath symbolizing victory. Five other wands surround him as he rides through a cheering crowd.

This is a card of success. Challenges and obstacles have been overcome and you are ready to reap the benefits of your hard work. If you are considering beginning a new project, now is the time to get things moving. This card is all about personal achievements, particularly if you have been working towards a goal for a long time, as finally you are able to see the finishing line. You will feel uplifted and proud of all you have done because, in some cases, you may have battled against the odds to get where you are now. This is a card of abundance, offering opportunity and success. You have reached a turning point and from here the only way is up!

You will have an air of confidence about you; nothing is too much of a challenge at this time, and your personal life is flowing beautifully. Be aware that the ego can be extremely powerful at this time, so be careful to keep your feet on the ground, as not everyone will share your happiness.

Reversed: Disputes, hurt pride, delays

Seven of Wands

Key words: Challenge, hard work, determination

Image: A man stands on top of a hill precariously near the cliff edge. He is defending his territory with determination. Note he is wearing different coloured shoes on each foot, implying imbalance.

You may feel raring to go with a new project or venture, but are apprehensive about the extent of the commitment involved in getting things started. However, if you don't try, you will never know. There is a sense of wanting to throw caution to the wind and this is fine, as long as you plan your strategy carefully.

If you are struggling to stay on top of things, this is a good time to rethink your situation and how you will find the strength to continue. There is great determination around you at this time. Nothing will faze you if you are in the right frame of mind and stay focused on your goal.

If there is a disagreement brewing and you feel the need to voice your concerns, be cautious and remember some battles are worth fighting for, while others just cause more trouble. Be honest with yourself about your motives in matters of conflict before taking action.

Reversed: Impatient, surrender, threatened

Eight of Wands

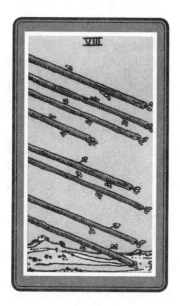

Key words: Action, conclusion, movement

Image: Eight budding wands move through the air. The sky is clear and the water calm, suggesting there are no obstacles in your path.

This card indicates swift action. If you have been waiting for change, it is about to happen. Things will begin to move at great speed, so ensure you are ready. This is very much a NOW card. There is no time for planning, as destiny is about to show you a new path. If events are already in motion, they will now gather momentum. The struggles and obstacles of the past have now cleared and you can look forwards to the next period of your life with joy and anticipation. If you have been dithering over a situation, it is time to take action.

You may be looking forwards to travelling opportunities, or even moving home. Movement is connected with the Eight of Wands. Surprise journeys may be offered to you, and life will be extremely busy during this period. This is not a time for dwelling on the past, as you have a bright future ahead of you. Don't be hasty in making major decisions; think before you act and everything will work out for the best.

Reversed: Disputes, arguments, delays

Nine of Wands

Key words: Persistence, struggle, turmoil

Image: A man stands alone supported by a wand, with eight additional wands planted firmly in the ground behind him, symbolizing a barrier. His head is bandaged showing he has been in battle. His expression is defensive as he gathers his strength.

You may be feeling you are moving two steps forwards and three steps back, and that whatever you try to achieve at the moment is proving difficult and challenging.

This is likely to be a difficult period in your life, as luck does not seem to be on your side. Don't despair; often situations such as this can be the beginning of our greatest achievements. When the situation turns in your favour, you will understand why so many obstacles were put in your path. It is important to remind yourself why you are doing all you can. You may be feeling defensive and that you need to protect yourself, but don't push away those with good intentions who may be able to help you.

If you are avoiding an issue that needs to be dealt with, it will not go away. Your intuition will guide you as to the best way to deal with the situation. Facing a difficult situation head-on will enable you to learn much more about yourself and allow your confidence to grow.

Reversed: Lack of mental strength, health issues, stress

Ten of Wands

Key words: Burden, struggle, overwhelmed

Image: A man struggles to walk to town while carrying ten heavy wands, which also block his view. He feels he has the weight of the world on his shoulders.

You are without a doubt doing too much, and pressure and commitments are taking their toll on you. You feel there is no pleasure in your life, just the daily grind. The saying 'all work and no play' certainly applies to your life at this time.

You may find it hard to say no. Therefore, certain people expect more and more from you. It is only because you appear so capable that your commitments continue to grow, resulting in added stress and burdens. It is time to look at your lifestyle choices. If you continue to ignore the pressures around you, then it is likely these will affect your health. When life feels like a struggle, it is important to recognize that you are in control, and can change whatever you need to. Harsh words sometimes need to be spoken in order to face the truth and release the pressure. You need to be kind to yourself and find a way to wind down. Formulate a plan as to how you can get your life back on track.

Reversed: Energy, shrewdness, avoiding responsibility

The suit of Cups (water)

Ace of Cups

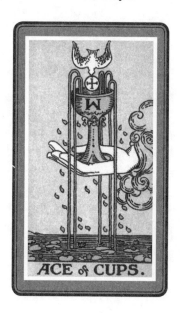

Key words: Joy, peace, emotional

Image: The Ace of Cups shows a hand emerging from a cloud holding a golden cup or chalice, which is overflowing with water. A dove of peace flies downwards holding a coin or disc.

This card marks the beginning of a new emotional journey. You are entering a peaceful period and leaving behind an emotional struggle. If you are able, this is a good time to heal old emotional scars, to forgive and forget and to let go of any negative baggage that is holding you back. This card asks that you look for the good in people, even those who may have hurt you in the past.

The Ace of Cups can also be associated with a new relationship. If you are not looking for love, then you are likely to receive happy news from someone close – maybe news of an engagement, a marriage or a birth.

Drawing a number one card, you may be feeling more creative than practical on a personal level. Your self-confidence is at a peak and you may feel ready to step outside your comfort zone and experience new challenges. Don't be shy, as you have a magnetic air about you at this time. Embrace the moment and take that step forwards that you have been thinking about for so long.

Reversed: Holding back, selfish, egotistical

Two of Cups

Key words: Love, partnerships, bonding

Image: A man and woman exchange cups possibly in a marriage ceremony. The symbol of Hermes hovers between them represented by two entwined snakes, which promises good luck. Above this, a lion's head symbolizing strength looks down on them.

Pay attention to this period in your life and do not dwell on the past. Expect opportunities to materialize, as the future looks bright. This is a good time for new partnerships, not only of a romantic kind, but also new friendships and business partnerships.

If you are looking for love, this card has all the right vibes for a special person to enter your life. This often materializes as a meeting of eyes across the room, because it can be a card of attraction rather than a meeting of minds. If you are experiencing difficulties in a current relationship, a decision will be made for the best. Ultimately, this is a good card for achieving harmony, even if sacrifices have to be made. If you are wondering whether you will ever meet your soul mate, the answer is yes. So, be sure to make the most of any social opportunities, as you never know where he or she might be!

Reversed: Heartache, separation, misunderstandings

Three of Cups

Key words: Friendship, celebration, unity

Image: Three women dressed in colourful robes dance and hold their cups high in celebration. Around their feet lie fruit and flowers, representing abundance.

Friendships reach a new level now and you feel supported. You are acknowledging the good fortune of having such people in your life. You may be thinking about joining a group or venturing into a situation that is dominated by females. If you have any fears, do not worry; this card suggests connections and friendships will be made.

This is a card of unity and good news. If you are waiting for news, it is likely to manifest now and to be in your best interest. I often see this card as the raising of a champagne glass – reason to celebrate and be joyful.

Music and dance can be prominent in your life, and you may be entering a phase of sociability, so don't make excuses for not participating, as there is a lot of fun to be had. You have experienced more than your fair share of emotional lows in the past, but now is your time to enjoy yourself and to have fun. More importantly, you have come through a difficult phase and you deserve the happiness this card brings.

Reversed: Gossip, an affair, emotional distress

Four of Cups

Key words: Losing interest, no effort, uninterested

Image: A young man sits beneath a tree with his legs crossed and his arms folded. He appears to be ignoring the cup being offered to him, or he may be sleeping. Either way, he seems oblivious to what is going on around him.

If you are trying to reach out to someone, it is likely they are not interested in what you have to offer at this time. There is no point in talking to someone who does not want to listen to reason.

Be aware of any opportunity being offered to you as initially, you may feel it is not right for you. However, this card encourages you to look deeper into the situation. You are feeling dismissive, but a great opportunity might be right under your nose. You may be limiting yourself. Open your eyes. It is a big, wide world out there so stop creating excuses why you can't do something, and find the energy to make life happen for you.

On a positive note, the Four of Cups could be you changing the way you deal with situations. Have you finally had the courage to say no and not feel pressured into doing things you do not wish to do? If this is the case, this is a card of strength and maturity – you are finding your inner confidence in order to become your own person.

Reversed: New goals, action, drive

Five of Cups

Key words: Loss, sadness, regret

Image: A solitary figure in a black cloak stands over three overturned cups, while behind him two cups stand upright. A stream, representing emotion, runs under a bridge. He is looking to the past unaware that the future offers stability.

This card suggests you have been through a period of pain or loss. The past issues are so prominent that you are unable to see the positive options awaiting you in the future. Dwelling on the past will not change anything nor put right what has happened. Life goes on, but allowing the negativity of a situation to consume your thoughts will only delay the healing process. You must find a way to let go. The longer you hold on to what has passed, the more bitterness and resentment will fester, and you will miss any opportunities that may be presented to you.

Your future is full of potential, so don't look back – what is done is done. Whatever choices you made in the past were right for you at that time, and there is no point focusing on decisions that have not gone your way.

Ignore the regret and loss of times gone by and focus on the promise of the future. If you have not experienced the energy of this card, be forewarned: feeling gratitude for all that you have is the best way to deal with the Five of Cups.

Reversed: New beginnings, hope, moving forwards

Six of Cups

Key words: Harmony, reunion, good relationships

Image: A young boy meets a female child in the village square and offers her flowers, symbolizing a gesture of friendship. This card is dominated by the colour yellow, which signifies happiness.

This suggests all is good in your world; relationships appear solid and there is an air of security around you. There is a shift in established relationships for the better, obstacles have been overcome and a mutual understanding has been reached. Outside of partnerships, friendship and family matters may take priority now. You may need to make a phone call, send an e-mail, or write a letter to an old friend, as someone is feeling neglected and contact from you will make all the difference.

Old friendships may rekindle under the influence of the Six of Cups and someone you have not seen for a long time may well pop back into your life. This is a time for positive reflection on the past, and childhood memories may come to the fore. Accept the good from the past and welcome this energy into your future.

If you have adult children, there may be news of a pregnancy or birth, or you may find yourself in the company of children.

Reversed: Disappointing friendships, stuck in the past

Seven of Cups

Key words: Illusion, shadow self, over-active imagination

Image: Seven cups appear to be floating on clouds. Six are filled with both positive and negative items; a cloth covers the seventh. The dark shadow of a man looks on.

This is a card of temptation, which is likely to lead to regret if you allow fantasy to overtake reality. It is also the card of the dreamer, and the saying 'If it looks too good to be true, it probably is' springs to mind and should be heeded. Conflicts between your dreams and fears are at the forefront of your mind. Do not rush decisions. If you do, you will only find yourself seeing what you choose to, and will neglect to weigh up the actual pros and cons.

This card suggests you are faced with a challenge, or perhaps you are tempted to do something that you know is wrong. You need to pull back and look at the situation without clouded judgement. You have choices, in fact, probably too many, but you need to take a step back and think clearly before moving forwards. Making the wrong decision will have consequences in the long-term. If you are thinking about having an affair, think again. The risk of getting caught is high.

Reversed: Will power, temptation, determination

Eight of Cups

Key words: Moving on, weariness, abandonment

Image: A man walks away from eight stacked cups over a rocky terrain and does not look back. The sun and the moon high in the sky represent darkness and light, a time to rebalance both materially and spiritually.

It is time to move on. It may be that you have been through a difficult period, and there is an air of disappointment around you. Nothing is forever and sometimes choices are challenging. However, a situation that has been draining you for some time now seems beyond repair, and the only way forwards is to break from the negative cycle that has been so prominent in your life for too long. You may not embrace the idea of change, but it will be beneficial in the long run.

This card warns you to be on your guard, as it can shake the foundations of all you know and wake you from a state of complacency. It encourages you to make the changes you need to create a better future for yourself. On a physical level, you may be changing jobs, moving home or leaving a relationship, and it is quite normal for there to be an air of concern and anticipation around you, but you have reached the end of a cycle and new doors will soon be opening.

Reversed: Looking for fulfilment, seeking pleasure

Nine of Cups

Key words: Contentment, good luck, good health

Image: A man sits on a wooden bench with his arms crossed looking contented. Nine cups form an arch behind him.

This is a card of good luck and it is often referred to as the 'wish' card. Luck is on your side and the outlook is good. Under the influence of the Nine of Cups, you can achieve anything. Naturally, everything should be done in moderation, but you can afford to push the boat out and expect a positive response.

You may be feeling extravagant or have an urge to indulge yourself, probably by eating and drinking more than is good for you. Occasionally, this does no harm, but don't overdo it, or you will have to deal with the unpleasant consequences.

It is time to look back on what you have achieved in the past, and to take pride in the solid foundation you have built for the future.

With this card, it is sometimes said that you need to be careful what you wish for as you just might get it. Make plans and dare to dream, as it is likely you will achieve your desired outcome.

Reversed: Materialism, illness, greed

Ten of Cups

Key words: Joy, peace, family

Image: A blissful scene of peace and harmony showing a family: a couple with two young children playing by their side. Ten cups are displayed in the arch of a rainbow, signifying all is well. The background is lush and fertile.

This is a card of happiness, joy and family unity. It can indicate a new relationship or established relationships reaching new levels of contentment. There is a sense of stability. Family relationships appear calm and without tension. If you are experiencing any family conflict, now is the time to settle disputes, as it is highly likely the outcome will benefit all involved.

You feel a sense of inner peace. Perhaps you have experienced some difficult times recently, but at long last you are feeling happy with your current situation. This is a very joyful phase in your life and if you are dealing with any issues, loose ends will soon be tied up and you can enjoy the peace that will ensue.

There is an air of calm around you; everyone close to you is well, and life is good. If you are thinking about making any major changes, trust your intuition. Your skills are finely tuned at the moment; allow yourself to be guided by your inner feelings and your circumstances will only get better.

Reversed: Broken dreams, misguided judgement

Chapter 5

Reading the Cards and Intuitive Interpretations

As it can be difficult for beginners to get to grips with the symbolism of the cards, we will concentrate on the pictures and work visually with your intuition to get you reading quickly and confidently.

When looking at any card in the deck, be aware of the colours in the card. Does red spell danger? Is yellow happiness, green healing, blue emotion? What do they mean to you? What are you sensing? Is the main image speaking to you? Is it telling you a story? Look at the background. We are often distracted by the main image on the card, but sometimes the answers lie in what is happening around and behind this. Each time you look at a Tarot card you will see and sense something new. Allow your intuition to flow and guide you and you will rarely be wrong.

Let us look at a few Minor Arcana cards in detail.

Nine of Pentacles

A woman stands in a vineyard. The vines are plentiful with red grapes symbolizing abundance. She is dressed in a luxurious yellow robe. She is self-confident and assured. This lady has accomplished much in her life and appears to be self-sufficient and independent. She is a woman of wealth and therefore, a lady of leisure who is enjoying the fruits of her past labour. The bird on the glove of her left hand is a falcon, indicating she has mastered her skills. Her right hand rests upon a Pentacle, signifying she embraces her wealth and success. There is a small snail at her feet and as snails carry their homes on their backs, this is a symbol of security. We assume the house, or possibly castle, in the background belongs to her. The two trees, one either side of her, represent balance. She has allowed her dreams and desires to manifest.

Intuitively you will sense this is a positive card. When you analyse the details, certain symbols will call to you. Don't worry if all that comes to mind is a word or a sentence; allow yourself to go with it and let the message flow.

Seven of Wands

A man stands on the edge of a cliff, appearing to be protecting his territory. He stands defensively, holding a wand across his body as if he is either ready for battle, or in a position to protect himself. He wears odd shoes, suggesting an imbalance in his thoughts and ideas. He straddles a small stream and, as water signifies emotional issues, perhaps he is hoping the problem will float away so he may not have to deal with it. The colour blue, which is the colour of communication, surrounds him. Perhaps you are holding back to avoid confrontation. The card suggests a need to take control of a situation.

Three of Swords

Three swords pierce a red heart suspended in the air. The weather is stormy, the clouds dark and the rain falls. This card suggests rejection in love, and feeling heartbroken and unable to see any light at the end of the tunnel due to the grief and darkness that surround you. The image within the card is simple yet speaks a thousand words. However, remember that clouds clear, weather changes and whatever sorrow this card might have in store, the situation will heal and pass.

Nine of Cups

A heavily framed man sits on a wooden bench, appearing prosperous, well fed and happy. His red hat symbolizes an active mind. The predominantly yellow background is the colour of intellect, which suggests he has achieved his status in life through confidence and strategy. Nine cups have been arranged behind him in a perfect arch, indicating this is someone who is careful, meticulous and precise. The colour blue represents communication. He does not worry about confronting issues, as he did not get where he is today without being confident. His yellow shoes suggest he is a quick thinker.

Tarot tip
Select a key word (or words) that triggers the strongest response you have to each of the cards. Associating key words with the images representing the cards will greatly help you to remember and understand their meanings.

More about card interpretation

By studying a card in detail, more and more images within the card come alive. When doing a reading, some of these images will feel more important than others. Allow your eyes to be drawn where they need to be, because this is where your psychic skills will start to work without you even realizing. It may be that you read a card and wonder where the information has come from, as often this information is above and beyond the meaning of the cards. This is a sure sign that you are connecting with the Higher Realms.

Tarot is a wonderful tool to help you develop your psychic ability and the more you trust your Tarot cards the more your intuition will flow. I will discuss more about psychic development and Tarot in Chapter 8.

The Minor Arcana at a glance

Here is a guide to help you learn the meanings of the Minor Arcana cards:

	Wands/Batons – fire		Cups – water
Ace	Fertility	Ace	Abundance
II	Achievement, new ideas	II	Love, good business
III	Seeking new adventure	III	Celebration
IV	Freedom, joy, balance	IV	Doubt, defensiveness
V	Disagreement	V	Disappointment
VI	Good news, victory	VI	Past influences
VII	Purpose, success	VII	Foolish whims
VIII	Sudden progress	VIII	Change of direction
IX	Expectations of difficulties	IX	Contentment
X	Unrealistic pressures	X	Happiness, joy

	Swords – air		Pentacles/Coins – earth
Ace	Great determination	Ace	Prosperity
II	Stalemate	II	Juggling life or money
III	Absence, sorrow	III	Skill in trade or work
IV	Temporary seclusion	IV	Hoarder
V	Destruction of others	V	Material trouble
VI	Trip or journey through difficulties	VI	Generosity
VII	Deception, dishonesty	VII	Success, growth
VIII	Restriction, turmoil	VIII	Diligence
IX	Anxiety over loved one	IX	Accomplishment
X	Sadness, misfortune, turning point	X	Prosperity, security

Chapter 6

The Court Cards

There are sixteen Court cards in a Tarot deck. Each suit (Pentacles, Swords, Wands and Cups) has four Court cards: a Page, a Knight, a Queen and a King. These Court cards are also sometimes known as the Royal Arcana.

Tarot Court cards serve several purposes. They relate to the querent and can represent a specific person in your life, or signify someone new coming into your life. The Court cards are very real as they deal with personal energy. Often you can pick up information intuitively with the Court cards, as you are dipping into someone's psyche. If a reading is dominated by the Court cards, it is likely the querent is experiencing interference from others, which is stopping them from trusting their own judgement.

Pages

Pages are the lowest order of the Court. They are the messengers and, in a reading, they represent news of all kinds, such as new relationships or work opportunities. These Court cards symbolize communication. They can also signify dreaming of the past, of a time when life was easier and less stressful. Pages can relate to children or someone younger than you and can be male or female.

Knights

Knights symbolize young adults, who bring in a new and often exciting energy. They can bring action to a situation or sometimes encourage us to be patient. Knights have the ability to move things along with great speed as well as postponing events. A Knight turning up in a Tarot reading can signify great determination. A Knight can be either male or female.

Queens

Queens represent mature women – sometimes our mothers or someone older than us. The Queen has a great deal of wisdom, gained throughout her life. She is very knowledgeable and is emotionally strong. She can offer good counsel as well as holding her own in a disagreement. The Queen is always a female.

Kings

Kings signify mature men. They can be a father figure or someone in authority such as a teacher, or someone you might seek advice from. The King has an air of strength about him. He is as wise as the Queen, but holds more authority and can sometimes appear intimidating.

Pages

Page of Pentacles (earth)

Key words: Devotion, new opportunities, financial gains

Image: A young man stands alone in a field, holding a bright Pentacle in his hand. The scene behind him looks fertile and new growth surrounds him.

A financial opportunity or offer may be on the horizon and a new journey is about to begin. If you have been working on a project, you will now begin to see the benefits of your time and effort coming to fruition. This is a good time to start planning, as the energy is potent and your enthusiasm high. Often, the Page of Pentacles appears when you have been doing too much daydreaming and not taking enough action. There is an ambitious streak in you and a desire to achieve more in your life. This is the time to move your projects and ideas forwards to make them reality. Whatever happens, be prepared for change, as you could be reconnecting with your inner child and seeking a different lifestyle. Change may take a physical or spiritual form.

The Page of Pentacles tends to have brown or black hair, and blue or hazel eyes.

Reversed: Wasteful, rebellious, bad news

Page of Swords (air)

Key words: Alert, mental ability, study

Image: A young man stands on a rocky surface, holding his sword in the air. You can see the clouds around him and his hair blowing in the wind, symbolic of air energy.

The Page of Swords is an intelligent young man, who is kind, thoughtful and will fight his corner if he feels there is an injustice.

This could also be a person who will argue the odds with passion even though they might be wrong. His ideas can change from day to day and, although he is enterprising, he may find it difficult to focus on his goal. He is easily distracted. However, once he finds the path that suits his needs, he is fully committed to see things through to the end. You may well be thinking about a new avenue of study, because the Page of Swords is keen to explore different subjects. His message may also indicate that there might be a delay in circumstances or there is a feeling of disappointment around you.

If there is an injustice, this card indicates you will not leave a stone unturned to find out the truth. Although sensitive in nature, the Page of Swords is ruthless when standing up for his rights or those of others. This Page tends to have brown hair and brown eyes.

Reversed: Cunning, non-committal, full of hot air

Page of Wands (fire)

Key words: Adventure, new beginnings, discovery

Image: A well-dressed young man stands in the middle of a barren terrain, holding his wand as he recites his dreams and desires.

This person is a free spirit: fun loving and a good friend who does not want to be restricted by commitments. He looks into the distance, seeking his options. He is ready for a new journey and yearns for excitement and challenges. This is always a positive card, as he is the bearer of good news, which is often connected with family announcements.

There is an urge to be spontaneous when this card appears. If you have been feeling in a rut, things are likely to change.

You are entering a period in which you will experience a new lease of life, and feel energized and ready for action. This is a good time to make progress. You may be emerging from a difficult phase in your life, but you will begin to see an improvement as issues start to be resolved ready for a new positive phase. There could also be a new love interest or person entering your life, who will become a trusted friend and companion. The Page of Wands tends to have blonde or red hair, and blue or hazel eyes.

Reversed: Instability, setbacks, depression

Page of Cups (water)

Key words: Creativity, new ventures, contemplation

Image: A young man appears to be standing on a beach holding a golden cup. As he attempts to drink from it a fish appears, the message being always to expect the unexpected.

This is the card of the dreamer, someone who has a caring and kind nature. They may have their head in the clouds and can be overly sensitive, but they are also intuitive and extremely creative when they finally get down to work. This card can signify the beginning of a new creative venture.

The Page of Cups is also sometimes known as the card of proposals – not necessarily marriage proposals, but also business offers and opportunities that can change your life for the better. As a dreamer, it is wise to weigh up options before making big decisions and refrain from allowing your desires to overrule logic and practicality.

The Page of Cups brings news of a pregnancy, birth, marriage or a happy family gathering. You may be feeling over-emotional right now. It is time to face situations that you have been avoiding. If you are not used to showing your emotions, you may find you can't stop the feelings flowing.

The Page of Cups tends to have light brown hair, and blue, brown or hazel eyes.

Reversed: Selfishness, lack of imagination, immaturity

Knights

Knight of Pentacles

Key words: Methodical, endurance, material world

Image: A Knight sits on a stationary plough horse. The fields around him appear barren, and the Knight seems to be considering his options before moving forwards.

The Knight of Pentacles can be one of life's plodders. This card lacks adventure and every decision is based on a process of careful logic. He considers everything before taking action, and can take so long weighing up the pros and cons and coming to a decision that the moment passes without him.

He is serious in nature and, in some ways, behaves in a manner older than his years suggest. With great planning comes a lack of spontaneity. There is a sense of boredom when this card appears. However, you are approaching a turning point with the opportunity to release yourself from your current situation. This card can represent someone consumed with financial concerns and worries. If you are lacking funds, rewards will come through hard work and enterprise. Alternatively, if you have abundant funds, you may be unwilling to spend as money and material value have overtaken your good sense. Although you may be carrying a lot of responsibility at the moment, you are coping remarkably well. You may now be feeling more assertive; this is a good time to be productive and to begin new projects.

Reversed: Boredom, Lack of interest, stuck

Knight of Swords

Key words: Action, argumentative, haste

Image: A Knight rides a white horse at speed while wielding his sword. Clouds gather, but he is focused on what is ahead of him. There is an air of aggression about him.

This card has a forceful energy. The Knight of Swords is powerful and full of 'get up and go', as he acts with speed in any event or situation. Often, he does not weigh up his options before charging into a situation. He is also occasionally thoughtless and cares only for his own needs and not those of others. He believes he is always right and can be argumentative, forcing his opinions on others.

On a positive note, this card can indicate a light-bulb moment, a time when taking action to get something moving feels right. Once you connect with this energy, there will be no stopping you. However, patience and planning are required, as you will feel everything needed to be done yesterday, but cutting corners to achieve a quick result is something you may regret in the future.

It is important at the moment to keep your emotions under control and not enter any conflicts, as your mood will be irrational and arguments may flare up. You love to talk and be the centre of attention, but pick your moments carefully.

If you have a habit of overthinking things, now is the time for less dithering and more action.

Reversed: Abandonment of ideas, lack of communication

Knight of Wands

Key words: Energy, vision, courage

Image: The Knight of Wands sits confidently astride his rearing horse, ready for his journey. He appears to be in a desert, working in the heat and the barren surroundings.

This is a card of action, speed, motivation and inspiration. You may feel that, at long last, things are about to get moving, that obstacles have been removed and a breakthrough is possible. Situations that appeared to be at a standstill will now flow with ideas and solutions.

As a person, the Knight of Wands can be aggressive, argumentative and over-confident. If you are dealing with a potentially volatile situation involving such a person, you may find yourself feeling intimidated and will have to work hard in standing up for your principles and what you believe to be true. Ensure you have all the facts before rushing headlong into a situation that will require more energy than is really needed.

This is a creative time and you may feel impulsive and therefore perhaps not take the time to be aware of all of your options. This card can also indicate entering a relationship too quickly. Try to take things slowly. If everything is in the right place, it will flow.

Reversed: Doubtful, lack of confidence, frustration

Knight of Cups

Key words: Love, new romance, creativity

Image: A young man on a white horse carries a golden cup. The horse is gently trotting towards a small stream, water being the symbol of emotions.

You may be about to encounter a new love in your life, or perhaps an ongoing relationship is about to reach a new level. This is a gentle card and the messenger will deliver some good news. If you are concerned about a situation, follow your intuition because this card connects with the heart. Although we often warn against allowing our emotions to rule our decisions, this card is the exception.

You may feel you are shouldering a lot of responsibility at the moment; however, even if the burden feels heavy, you are coping remarkably well. This is a good time to be productive, especially with projects you have been thinking about starting, or by working with something you are passionate about. Make sure the goals you are setting are within your reach, and you have not taken on more than you can deal with. This is sometimes the card of a 'people pleaser'. Ensure your boundaries are where you want them to be and not under someone else's control.

Reversed: Trickery, moodiness, over-emotional

Queens

Queen of Pentacles

Key words: Mother, security, financially abundant

Image: The Queen of Pentacles sits upon her throne, holding a large coin, surrounded by a lush landscape representing the abundance of Mother Earth.

If you are seeking support, your mother or a mother figure is waiting in the wings. She may be someone you look up to and respect, such as an employer, a teacher or a doctor. Whoever she is, she has your best interests at heart. She has a nurturing and kind nature. If you have been through a difficult period, you can share your concerns with her without fear of judgement.

The Queen of Pentacles reminds us of our own path and of the need for independence and security. Finding a career path that can provide for you, or gaining a better-paid job, may be in the forefront of your mind. Your financial security is vital to you now, and you need to look for ways to make this reality. Home and family are also especially important, and maybe you have recently overindulged financially. However, this is a positive card and, if you are able to take control of your finances, it will not take long to get back on your feet.

Reversed: Overly dependent, neglect, selfishness

Queen of Swords

Key words: Privacy, perception, sadness

Image: The Queen of Swords sits on a throne facing to the right. She holds a sword upwards in a defensive manner and averts her gaze. The clouds gather around her and her thoughts are deep.

The Queen of Swords is a private person, who does not need, or want, to be around people. However, if you are a friend of the Queen of Swords, you will be a friend for life. She is very selective about who she allows into her inner circle but, once you have a good relationship with her, she will do anything for you.

She often does not think before she speaks and will tell you exactly how it is. She is very judgemental, but cannot take criticism herself. She has a razor-sharp mind and tongue. This card can also occasionally relate to a woman who is going through a loss, such as divorce or bereavement.

You are advised to look at both sides of a volatile situation. If you do not allow yourself to be flexible, you may end up being in the wrong. If there is an argument brewing, you are advised to stay impartial, otherwise you will find yourself involved whether or not you choose to be.

Reversed: Cold-hearted, cruel, narrow-minded

Queen of Wands

Key words: Energy, vibrancy, independent

Image: The Queen of Wands sits upon her throne, a wand in one hand and a sunflower in the other. At her feet sits a black cat, symbolizing magic.

There is an air of confidence about you when you pull this card, and you will feel ready to take on the world. If you are looking for work or promotion, now is the time to put yourself forwards as your energy levels are high and people are attracted to you. You may be thinking about taking on a new challenge. You need to keep moving forwards without hesitation. Being inactive does not sit well with you. Joining a group is a good idea, although it is likely you will end up running it.

This is the time to break out of your comfort zone and show the world what you are made of. The desire to achieve great things, to become a leader and step out of a rut, will feel important to you now. You have a very determined nature and nothing will stop you reaching your goal. Once you know what you want to do, you will move mountains to achieve this. If you have someone in need around you, you have the power and the personality to help him or her move forwards. You are a generous friend and give others the confidence to achieve their dreams and desires.

Reversed: Vengeful, aggressive, unreasonable

Queen of Cups

Key words: Intuition, emotional calm, compassion

Image: The Queen of Cups sits upon her throne, surrounded by water. The closed cup has handles of angel wings, and the blue sky is cloudless, symbolizing clarity.

This is a card of emotional stability. Whatever you have been through in the past, you can now relax. Emotional upheavals are behind you, and you are feeling confident and strong. This card can relate to your mother, or perhaps to yourself if you are a mother. If this is the case, your children may be seeking advice and need guidance at this time.

When this card appears, you may be dealing with someone else's emotional problems, and they are looking to you to help them get through a difficult time. You are trustworthy and kind, and through your own past experiences you are able to give gentle but firm advice.

This is a highly intuitive card and you need to take notice of your inner feelings. You are a natural healer, even psychic. Allow these feelings to surface, and you will realize how powerful and strong your senses are. However, be aware that when major decisions have to be made, you are tuning in to what you feel is right and not what you want to be right. You can often bring too much logic to a situation and therefore confuse the issue. Try to trust your own instincts.

Reversed: Co-dependency, insecurity, emotional

Kings

King of Pentacles

Key words: Security, power, business

Image: The King of Pentacles sits upon his throne holding a coin and a sceptre, surrounded by the abundance of the land. A castle sits behind him, symbolic of his success and security.

If life has been a roller coaster ride recently you will now begin to see things slowing down. Things are about to change for the better and there is a sense of stability and financial security around you. Investments are solid and your feet are firmly on the ground.

If you are dependent on another person, then their luck is about to change and you will benefit from this. If you are in a relationship, you will feel safe and secure as things can only improve at this time. If you are thinking about moving home or making an investment, negotiation is the key, and it is likely you will get a very good deal. Issues around finances are strong and if you have had money worries in the past, that is where they will stay because now is a time to benefit from some clever decisions.

The King of Pentacles may be a person who will advise you on investments or a prospective employer. He is trustworthy and experienced in his field. However, he will expect total commitment from you to achieve a goal. He did not become successful without hard work and determination.

Reversed: Controlling, greedy, lack of commitment

King of Swords

Key words: Intelligence, truth, integrity

Image: The King of Swords sits upon his throne with a sword held rigidly in his right hand. His gaze is direct and determined. The birds in the landscape behind him represent the element of air and thought.

It is time to cut through illusion and view any unresolved issues with truth and integrity. This is the time to be courageous as justice is on your side. The important focus at this time, in order to resolve unwanted issues, is to stay detached and not allow your emotions to overwhelm logic. You may need to seek advice from an expert to help you bring an issue to a conclusion. If this is the case, the King of Swords will be of great benefit to you. If you need legal advice, this man will act as a strong and positive influence on your behalf.

Be aware of a male who can be very persuasive, as the King of Swords can be a charmer – someone who can talk his way in or out of any situation. If this relates to you, ensure you have a balanced opinion when involved in issues that have the potential to become heated.

When this card is drawn it reminds us that we should respect those who offer us advice. However, we should also be prepared to put forwards our own opinion on the matter.

Reversed: Injustice, obstinate, lack of confidence

King of Wands

Key words: Leader, business-like, entrepreneur

Image: The King of Wands holds a wand in his right hand, which is sprouting new shoots, symbolizing growth. His red cloak signifies fire energy.

This card represents new opportunities. It also relates to your creative energy. He is a risk-taker but, as a leader, the risks are measured. Although he may appear reckless, he rarely takes uncalculated chances.

There is an opportunity for change around you, particularly connected to work and any ambitious projects that may be close to your heart. The determination of this card will guide you in making the correct choices, in engaging with the right people and allowing your drive and enthusiasm to move full steam ahead. You will be feeling particularly motivated around this time. The norm is not enough for you now and you feel ambitious. Do not be afraid to consider your options. There is a brighter future for you if you are brave enough to grab it with both hands.

If you have met the King of Wands in the romantic sense, be aware that, although he is great fun, he is unlikely to stay committed to one relationship. He loves the outdoors, is adventurous and will live life to the full.

Reversed: Intolerant, impulsive, unscrupulous

King of Cups

Key words: Emotional security, kindness

Image: The King of Cups sits upon his throne, which is surrounded by rough waters. The jumping fish in the background symbolizes that our emotions are changeable. A ship, battling with the choppy waters, can be seen behind him on the left.

The King of Cups is a symbol of emotional security. He may be a family man, a lover or a kind soul who cares about others. He takes on responsibility without feeling burdened and overcomes obstacles in his stride. When dealing with the King of Cups in a professional context, note that he is level-headed and can balance logic and emotional issues with your best interests at heart.

You may be thinking about your dreams and desires and how you can manifest them. Under the influence of this card you are advised to get started, even just by taking the smallest step. You need to begin somewhere.

You are highly creative and should trust your intuition more. Try not to take any negativity to heart, as you can be over-sensitive, and need to learn to be stronger in confrontational situations.

If you are looking for love, this can be a very good period for you, as this card can often signify a new relationship and potential lover.

Reversed: Scandal, manipulative, controlling

Court cards at a glance

Card	Interpretation
King of Pentacles	Successful leader, business acumen, loyal friend
Queen of Pentacles	Prosperity, wellbeing, extreme comfort
Knight of Pentacles	Mature, responsible, reliable, patient
Page of Pentacles	Study, scholarship, respect for knowledge
King of Swords	Professional man; represents justice, force and power
Queen of Swords	Woman of sadness, bearer of slanderous words
Knight of Swords	Young man symbolizes bravery and skill
Page of Swords	Person who uncovers the unknown or the less obvious
King of Wands	Mature, wise and friendly, well educated
Queen of Wands	Sympathetic and understanding person
Knight of Wands	Departure, journey, advancement into the unknown
Page of Wands	Faithful and loyal person; trusted friend
King of Cups	Man of responsibility, kindly and responsible
Queen of Cups	Warm-hearted person, devoted wife, mother
Knight of Cups	An invitation or opportunity may arise
Page of Cups	Willing to offer services towards specific goal

Tarot tip

The Court cards have more variability than the other cards in Tarot because they reflect real people and often bring with them direct messages. They can represent people from the past or present, or in the future.

Part III

BRINGING IT ALL TOGETHER

In this part of the book you'll learn about different Tarot spreads, how to link the cards together during a reading and how to ask questions.

Chapter 7

Readings and Spreads

Shuffling the cards

It is important that, before you start reading the cards, you give your deck a really good shuffle. It may be that the first few readings are dominated by a particular suit, and if this is the case, shuffle again. Shuffling the deck is a ritual. Therefore, you, as the reader, should shuffle until it feels right to stop. If you are asking a question of the cards, ask this quietly in your mind while you shuffle. Your intuition will tell you when the cards are in the right place for you, and you will instinctively stop. If you are reading for another person, again shuffle the cards first, then hand them to the querent and ask them to continue shuffling until it feels right to them to stop.

Laying the cards

If you have had Tarot readings in the past, you might have noticed that no two readers lay or interpret the cards the same. Some readers lay the cards face down and some face up. To be honest, this is an entirely personal choice. I prefer to lay the cards face up, and as I place each card, I am already interpreting the meaning in my mind and linking the cards together before I begin vocalizing the reading. Sometimes one card will talk to me more than others, and I'll know that the energy of that card needs to be focused on. The other important factor when laying the cards is the position of each card. To start, I will show you simple spreads in which we read from left to right, but even when using this technique you may still be drawn to a particular card laid further on in the spread. Listen to those insights, as they will guide you.

Linking cards together

As a beginner, the most difficult part of reading the cards is linking them together. You may know the meaning of each card individually, but how do they flow into each other? A really good way to practise interpreting the cards and linking them together is to lay 5 or 6 cards face down. Pick up the first card and quickly give an interpretation, then the next card, then the next, and so on. The skill here is speed – you can go back and add layers to the reading, but when you intuitively add an interpretation to a card and move on, your left-brain will not have time to allow you to question your flow.

Tarot can literally guide you on any issue, so always bear in mind the question asked. There is never a situation in which the cards do not link together, even if it seems like the most bizarre combination. In a reading, some cards have a greater impact than others, and they might not be part of the Major Arcana. Do not try to think too hard, simply allow your intuition to flow. If you allow logic to consume your thoughts, the reading will be difficult to interpret. Sometimes holding a card in your hand for a few seconds to connect with it will get the intuitive juices flowing. As with many situations in life, the more you trust your instincts and practise, the easier reading Tarot will become.

What does it mean if a suit dominates the reading?

Providing you have shuffled your cards well, when you lay them you will get a true reading. It is important to scan the cards quickly and be aware if a suit dominates the spread. If it does, this will give you a good indication of the querent's issues. For example, if a spread is dominated by Cups (water), then we know the querent is too emotionally involved to deal with a situation without their heart ruling their head. If the reading is dominated by Pentacles (earth), they are not being flexible and their feet are planted too firmly on the ground. If it is dominated by Swords, (air), the querent is thinking about the situation far too much and not taking action. And finally, if the reading is predominately Wands (fire), then they are rushing in headfirst without weighing up the consequences of their actions.

Sequence of reading the cards

Unless you are following a spread that has specific placements, the usual sequence of reading the cards is from left to right. If you are reading a spread with a particular number of cards, for instance a three-card spread or a seven-card spread, and you complete the reading with a card that leaves the querent's question in limbo, then lay another card. For example, imagine having the last card as the Hanged Man. You cannot leave the reading literally hanging there! It may be that you have to lay three or four additional cards to complete the reading, and if this is the case, then do so.

How can Tarot benefit you?

Tarot is a great aid for helping you find solutions to your problem, and assisting you in making decisions that are right for you. It is also a wonderful tool for self-exploration and personal growth. I recommend that you pull one card a day to use for meditation, quiet contemplation and as a guide for the day. Aside from giving you additional practice with the cards, it will also benefit you to become more aware of the various energies and possibilities surrounding you.

Meditating with Tarot

This is a very powerful technique and will not only help you to connect with the energy of the card, but will allow you to experience particular cards in great depth. Quiet your mind and study every aspect of the card you have pulled for a few minutes, then close your eyes and imagine the card becoming larger until it is the size of a door. Then see yourself stepping inside the card and speaking with the main character. If this feels right and comfortable for you, you will be able to explore the card from 'behind the scenes'.

Tarot tip
This is a good time to re-read Chapter 1: The Basic Rules of Tarot. Then unseal your deck, begin to shuffle and get started with the spreads.

Three-card Tarot spreads for personal development

Here are a group of three-card spreads, focused on personal development. Follow the same process for each of them.

Always shuffle the cards for each question. Ask the question in your mind then lay the top card face up from left to right. Repeat the process with the next question, and then again for the third question.

Valuing myself

1. What do I need to let go to allow me to grow?

2. What aspect do I need to focus on?

3. What needs to be my priority?

My path

1. What do I need to change about my life?

2. What guidance do I need to be aware of?

3. What do I need to take into consideration?

Becoming successful

1. What holds me back from being successful?

2. What will inspire me?

3. What advice do I need to create success?

Karmic lesson

1. What negative attribute did I bring in from a past life?

2. How can I release this for my best interest?

3. How will this help me in the future?

Who am I? (Court cards only)

1. Who was I in a past life?

2. Whose energy do I carry now?

3. Who do I have the potential to be?

The four-card spread

Now try four-card spreads using the same process.

Movement

1. My current situation

2. Am I moving in the right direction?

3. What can I do to help my situation?

4. The outcome

Challenges

1. What do I need to know about my current challenge?

2. How can I resolve this quickly?

3. Is this challenge karmic?

4. How best can I deal with this?

Learning

1. What talent am I unaware of?

2. How do I proceed in learning this?

3. Is there a new opportunity for me?

4. Do I seek this or does it find me?

Dreams and obstacles

1. What is stopping me?

2. What motivates me?

3. What distracts me?

4. What will drive me to my goal?

Action

1. Is the time right for me to act on a situation?

2. How should I proceed for the best outcome?

3. What do I need to be aware of?

4. What will be the outcome?

The seven-card spread

This spread looks briefly at past issues and then moves on to deal with the current situation and the outcome. If the final card leaves you in limbo with a card that does not give guidance, lay another card (or two), so that you have a clear idea as to how you move forwards. The time-span for the outcome is usually within one year of the day of the reading.

The seven-card spread has a few different variations, and the most popular version is where the fourth card is used as the significator. In my experience, this has not always produced the most accurate reading and therefore, I personally prefer to read the cards from left to right.

My version is as follows:

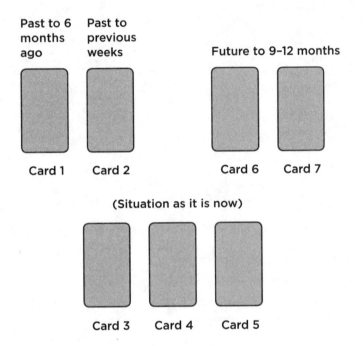

The ten-card spread – The Celtic Cross

The Celtic Cross is probably the most well known of all Tarot spreads. It is not the easiest of spreads to learn, as you need to remember what each position represents and, of course, the card meanings and how they relate to each position.

It is thought that this spread dates back to the 1800s, when Tarot was used only by the European travellers and gypsies, most of whom were very superstitious. They would lay the cards in the form of a Christian or Celtic Cross as a form of protection.

Interestingly, structured layouts were more common at that time than they are now. As Tarot has become more than just a tool for divination, in modern times we are more likely to 'throw' a few cards at a question rather than lay a particular spread.

Still, the Celtic Cross is a great way to master the cards and their meanings.

When using this spread it is not so important that the cards flow into each other, as in a Celtic Cross reading each card has a specific placement. However, each card is still influenced by what surrounds it.

If you have a particularly challenging situation, this spread will help you to deal with the issues in great depth. It will give you deeper insight into the causes the issue and how to move forwards. It is acceptable to lay an 11th card if you feel you need further clarification about the outcome.

With practice, this spread will become your friend, although initially, you may find that you have to keep referring to the placements. Once you master this spread you will not look back!

There are many variations of this particular spread. For consistency, this version of the Celtic Cross is the one most associated with the Rider Waite deck.

The Celtic Cross

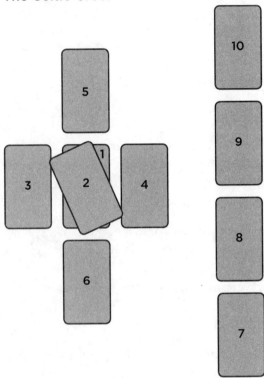

Card positions:

1. Experience to date
2. Where you are now
3. Hopes or fears
4. Recent past and long-term blocks
5. Obstacles
6. The near future

7. How the near future will evolve
8. New turns of events and/or unexpected changes
9. You in the future
10. Outcome or summary

Spiritual guidance reading

This spread has been developed to guide you along your spiritual path. The eight questions are designed to give a better understanding of the motivating factors involved. This layout relates to your spiritual growth. Shuffle the cards for each question, then lay the cards face up.

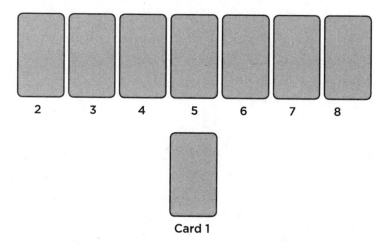

2   3   4   5   6   7   8

Card 1

Questions

1. Which card represents me right now?

2. How important is my spiritual path at this time?

3. What aspect of my life needs to be a priority?

4. What do I need to release in order to grow?

5. How will taking action affect me?

6. What guidance are my spirit guides offering me?

7. How do I proceed in developing my spiritual path?

8. Which card best represents me if I follow the advice given?

This is a reading you can do for yourself. It is a very good motivator when you are feeling low as it gives a clear picture of the positive action you need to take.

Chapter 8

Psychic Readings with Tarot

Many people ask if you have to be psychic to read the cards. The answer is no. Anyone can study the cards and learn their meanings. However, when we merge knowledge and intuition together, the messages can be powerful. Everyone has intuition; we are all born with it. It is a primal instinct but, unfortunately, many of us lose this sense when we are children, usually at around the age of seven. It is believed that our 'sixth sense' becomes stronger when we do psychic practice. Using your cards regularly will increase your spiritual awareness.

Even those who believe they have no psychic gift at all will discover, through reading the cards, that they are able to receive and offer information over and above the literal meaning of the cards. How many times have you talked yourself out of going with your gut feeling only to realize later that you made a mistake? Probably more often than you care to remember. When you learn to trust this primal instinct, it will guide you in making decisions that are right for you. It is the same with Tarot. Your sixth sense will awaken the more you practise Tarot and your readings will become more powerful.

We each connect with our psychic senses in different ways, such as clairaudience (clear hearing), clairvoyance (clear vision), clairsentience (clear feeling) and claircognizance (clear knowing). It is likely you will discover that one of these senses is stronger for you than others, but whatever your gift, learn to trust it. Clairvoyance as a term originates from the French word *claire*, which means 'clear', and *voyance*, 'seeing'. It literally means 'clear seeing'. It is quite common to 'see' images in your mind as you read the cards, but don't be alarmed – your sixth sense is waking up.

As you look at a card, allow your thoughts to flow – don't force the information. Note the colours in the card, the images, and examine the scenes behind the image. Allow something in the card to draw your eye, then the reading will evolve naturally.

Protection

When we work with psychic energy, we can inadvertently pick up negative energy. Psychic protection exercises can take less than a minute and should be used whenever you are consciously ready to work with spirit or psychic energy. Here are some easy and quick suggestions for protection.

Sit quietly until your breathing becomes even. Visualize a white light coming down from the heavens and washing over you. See this light as a barrier between you anything you do not invite into your space.

Light a white candle, and as you do so, state your intention and ask for protection for the work you are about to do.

If working with crystals, choose those you are drawn to and programme them to protect you from any harmful influences. Always wash the crystals after use.

Tarot tip
Burning incense, or using Ting-sha or a singing bowl, are powerful ways to cleanse the energy in the room before and after a reading.

How to ask questions

1. Shuffle your cards and think of a question.

Allow your intuition to guide you as to when to stop shuffling. Lay the top card but do not look at it. Hold it between your hands, tune into the energy of the card and ask what guidance you are being given to help find an answer to your question. When you have received the information, turn over the card and see what you have chosen. Now, using this card, think about the guidance you have received and how the card you have drawn relates to this. Whatever the card is, it will have an influence on your message and will give you additional information.

2. Yes or no

Often we just need a simple yes or no answer. While shuffling the deck ask the question in your mind. It is important that you ask the question so that the answer cannot be confused. For example, supposing you ask, 'Should I move house'? You may well move within the next five years or so. However, if this is a question of urgency, close the question by asking,

'Will I move within the next month'? This way, you have asked a direct question with a time-span. Shuffle the cards until it feels right to stop, and then lay the top card.

A general rule of Tarot is that even numbers are a yes, uneven ones are no. If the answer is not what you are expecting, look at the card as it will give you guidance on why now it not the right time. If it feels appropriate, lay another card or two to give you a clearer insight as to why you should wait.

3. Asking a question to someone who has passed over

Sometimes we need the comfort of knowing that our loved ones are close by. If you have a question to ask a deceased loved one, first find their archetype within the Court cards. For example, if you are trying to connect with a mother or grandmother, then use one of the Queens. For a Grandfather use a King; for a young person use a Knight; for a child, a Page card. You will intuitively be drawn to the energy of the card, which connects most closely with them. Lay that card upright in front of you and think about the person. You may feel the need to have a photograph of them next to the card.

Shuffle the remaining deck and, using the person's name (or Mum, Dad, Grandma, etc.), ask them to help guide you with your question. When you are ready, stop shuffling and lay the top card next to their Court card. You may feel the need to lay more. There is no right or wrong with this type of reading, the spread is complete when the question has been answered.

When you have finished the reading, thank them and re-shuffle the cards before you place them back in their cloth.

4. The voice within the card

This is a lovely exercise in which you shuffle and pull a card, then ignore the main feature within the card. Look at what is going on in the background, and look at the colours. Which one is dominating the card? Does the number of the card have a particular significance? Is the number calling you with a message about the number of days, weeks, months or years a situation will require to evolve? The voice in the card is the meaning beyond what we perceive to be normal within a reading. It is likely you will see symbols and images you had previously been unaware of. For instance, if there is water in the scene, is it calm or choppy? Could this be a message regarding an emotional issue? The voice in the card literally talks to you and tells you a story hidden behind the main character or image.

'Flying' cards

Sometimes when shuffling your deck a card flips spontaneously out of the pack. Yes, it is trying to get your attention. If this happens to one of my clients, I take the card and lay it on the table and ask them to continue shuffling so that I can lay a spread for them. At some point during the reading the 'flying' card will become significant and this will be focused on for a short period, as it will likely merge with the reading.

Occasionally a 'flying' card will have an important message for the querent and should be read as a one-card reading.

It is important you trust your intuition with a flying card as it often has an important, relevant message.

Often, if a client is nervous when shuffling, the cards are literally flying out all over the place or dropping to the floor. If this happens, put the cards back in the deck and ask the client to take his or her time and reshuffle, as it is highly unlikely that the dropped cards will be of any relevance to the reading.

The 'shadow' card

Just before you are ready to lay your cards for a reading, look at the bottom card, as occasionally this can be very relevant to the querent. This card is known as the 'shadow' card as it sometimes relates to a goal you are striving for but not able to take control of at this time. For example, if the shadow card is something positive such as the Sun card, then it is likely the querent is struggling to keep a balance in everyday life. If the shadow card is the Devil, they might be having difficulty letting go of the ties that bind them. If it is a Court card, it is possible that a third party is blocking their goals.

Often the shadow card gives us a message we do not want to hear. We know what we should be doing to achieve our goals, but we do not want to face the consequences of making the changes that are needed, which is why the card sits in the shadow.

However, the shadow card is not always relevant. Use your intuition and decide if the message is important enough to share. But it is always worth having a look, as it may well offer a significant message that will aid the reading.

Using an Oracle deck to complement a Tarot reading

With so many beautiful Oracle decks on the market, it is a nice idea when you have finished a reading, to pull a card from an Oracle deck. The difference between a Tarot deck and an Oracle deck is that Tarot cards will give you a balanced view of a situation whether good and bad, whereas Oracle cards tend to be mainly positive.

When you have completed your Tarot reading, shuffle your chosen Oracle cards and ask for one card to clarify and sum up your reading. Make a note of this card; it is likely to be highly relevant and inspirational.

Creating your own spread

It is really easy to create your own spread. Think about the questions you would like guidance on and write them down. Decide how many cards the spread will have and then design a unique layout for your reading.

Give your reading a name and write it in a journal (or a Tarot Book of Shadows) with the questions and a diagram of how the cards should be laid.

Over time, you will create a personal reference book of your spreads and questions. It may be advisable to have a spread for each topic, such as love, money, career and so on.

Chapter 9

Using a Significator

A significator is a card that you take from the deck to determine the energy of a person on whom the reading should focus. It can be you or another person. Not every spread uses a significator, but it can be helpful if you want to concentrate on a particular issue.

Generally, a standard significator for a man is often the Emperor, and for a woman the Empress. You could work out the birth card for the person and use the Major Arcana card with the corresponding number, or choose from the Court cards and use one of these as the significator.

Here is a sample reading dealing with a third party.

Think about the person with whom you have an issue and choose a card to represent them either from the Court cards or the Major Arcana. Lay this card at the top of the spread. Ask the following questions, shuffle and lay a card for each one.

How does this person affect my life?

Why do I allow this person to affect my life?

Do the cards advise me to confront this person?

How would this person react to me confronting them?

Would discussion resolve the problem?

Does this person understand the issue?

Will we resolve the problem peacefully?

Tarot tip
If you prefer to word the questions differently in the spreads or exercises in this book, please do. The examples included are meant as guidelines, and should be adapted to your specific needs.

The wonderful thing about Tarot is that you can ask the cards anything, including how to proceed in dealing with a particular problem. Using them as a significator is a way to bring a person into your reading without having them there. It will give you a greater understanding of their thoughts about a situation that involves you, but at the same time without asking anything about them personally, just how their attitude and presence affect you.

This is a good time to mention that it is not deemed ethical to do a distant Tarot reading for someone else without their permission.

Conclusion

Summing Up

Tarot is a powerful tool both for guidance and predicting the future. It is always important to remember that you have the choice to change the things in your life that you no longer need or want.

People often ask if a Tarot reading is set in stone, and of course it is not. You have free will, though it is highly likely you will recognize the advice and wisdom the cards offer, even if you focus on changing an outcome. Tarot will help and guide you to make both major and minor decisions. The cards never lie. It will tell us things we don't want to hear and bring us joyous news of the unexpected. If you receive news that you find challenging from a Tarot reading, look for the positive aspect of the message. It is always there. However you use your cards, always respect their energy.

Each one of us is on a unique journey, and the Tarot cards within a reading will change as our situations progress. Life is not always within our control, and when challenges overwhelm you, ask the cards for help. Heed their advice, then try to go with the flow – the cards will guide you on how to do this.

As you lay a spread, the cards pick up the vibration of where you are in your life right now. This will determine how things will pan out if you follow the current path. However, if you choose otherwise, as you are free to do, the cards will change. Always remember that you are in control of your own destiny.

Those who are fearful of Tarot need to understand that it is a wise friend. The reality is that Tarot is a set of 78 cards with pictures on them. The cards are wise – sometimes it is the readers who are not! Trust your instincts and always be responsible.

Enjoy learning Tarot and allow it to become your wise friend!

Resources

Online resources

www.tarotconference.co.uk
Information about the annual UK Tarot Conference in
London, and details about my ongoing workshops

www.theatlantisbookshop.com
The Atlantis Bookshop, London, for card decks and books
on all aspects of Tarot

www.aeclectic.net/tarot/
Aeclectic Tarot, for Tarot books, and reviews and images
of decks

www.tabi.org.uk
The Tarot Association of the British Isles

www.tarotschool.com
The Tarot School, New York:

www.thinkfilms.co.uk
Link to my short 3-D animation, *The World of Tarot*,
produced by Jeff Shephard

Books

365 Tarot Spreads: Revealing the Magic in Each Day, Sasha Graham (Llewellyn Publications, 2014)

The Tarot: The Origins, Meaning and Uses of the Cards, Alfred Douglas (Sheridan Douglas Press, 4th revised edition, 2007)

The Tarot Bible, Sarah Bartlett (Godsfield Press, 2009)

Tarot for Your Self: A Workbook for Personal Transformation, Mary K. Greer (New Page Books, 2002)

The Tarot Masters: Insights from the World's Leading Tarot Experts, Kim Arnold (Hay House UK, 2013)

Tarot Prediction & Divination: Unveiling Three Layers of Meaning, Susyn Blair-Hunt (Llewellyn Publications, 2011)

The Ultimate Guide to the Rider Waite Tarot, Johannes Fiebig & Evelin Burger (Llewellyn Publications, 2013)

ABOUT THE AUTHOR

Kim Arnold is a professional Tarot reader and teacher, and the founder of the prestigious UK Tarot Conference, an event that brings together some of the most exciting Tarot authors, artists and teachers from around the world. Having celebrated a decade of success, the conference continues to gather strength and is now rated as one of the best in the world.

Kim's passion continues to grow as she works tirelessly to enlighten people with the knowledge and wisdom of this ancient craft.

www.tarotconference.co.uk

Hay House Podcasts
Bring Fresh, Free Inspiration Each Week!

Hay House proudly offers a selection of life-changing
audio content via our most popular podcasts!

Hay House Meditations Podcast

Features your favorite Hay House authors guiding you through
meditations designed to help you relax and rejuvenate. Take
their words into your soul and cruise through the week!

Dr. Wayne W. Dyer Podcast

Discover the timeless wisdom of Dr. Wayne W. Dyer, world-
renowned spiritual teacher and affectionately known as "the
father of motivation." Each week brings some of the best
selections from the 10-year span of Dr. Dyer's talk show on
Hay House Radio.

Hay House Podcast

Enjoy a selection of insightful and inspiring lectures from Hay House Live
events, listen to some of the best moments from previous Hay House Radio
episodes, and tune in for exclusive interviews and behind-the-scenes audio
segments featuring leading experts in the fields of alternative health, self-
development, intuitive medicine, success, and more! Get motivated to live
your best life possible by subscribing to the free Hay House Podcast.

*Find Hay House podcasts on iTunes, or visit
www.HayHouse.com/podcasts for more info.*

HAY HOUSE
Look within

Join the conversation about latest products,
events, exclusive offers and more.

f Hay House UK

🐦 @HayHouseUK

📷 @hayhouseuk

🖤 healyourlife.com

We'd love to hear from you!